THERE ARE MORAL ABSOLUTES

HOW TO BE ABSOLUTELY SURE THAT CHRISTIANITY
ALONE SUPPLIES THE CONDITIONS FOR MORAL
CERTAINTY THROUGH PRESUPPOSITIONAL
APOLOGETICS

MICHAEL A. ROBINSON

Outskirts Press, Inc.
Denver, Colorado

There Are Moral Absolutes
How to Be Absolutely Sure That Christianity Alone Supplies All Rights Reserved
Copyright © 2007 Michael A. Robinson

Outskirts Press
http://www.outskirtspress.com

ISBN-10: 1-59800-766-1
ISBN-13: 978-1-59800-766-4

Library of Congress Control Number: 2006930479

Outskirts Press and the "OP" logo are trademarks belonging to
Outskirts Press, Inc.

Printed in the United States of America

THERE ARE MORAL ABSOLUTES!

How to Be Absolutely Sure That Christianity Alone Supplies
The Conditions For Moral Certainty Through
Presuppositional Apologetics
Pastor Michael Allen Robinson

CONTENTS

I dedicate this book to my mother and father: they taught me right from wrong, and lived a life towards God. I offer this work to my dear Lord Jesus Christ, to my Savior, for without His love and power I can do nothing.

CHAPTER 1
CHRISTIANITY: THE SOURCE OF UNIVERSAL ETHICS

Many ideologies and religions offer moral laws, but they are inconsistent and cannot be justified within the system itself. Some people believe it is right to lie and murder in order to promote their agenda. To a consistent atheist, the concept of nonmaterial law is nonsensical. The concept of moral law does not come from the material world, therefore to the consistent atheist, the notion of an absolute moral law does not exist. The only consistent and righteous moral system for the individual is Christian law. It can be justified and it is impossible for it not to be true because Christianity alone supplies the necessary preconditions for absolute moral law.

Many skeptics have admitted that they embraced Darwinism so they could live in complete sexual freedom and toleration. These profligates despised the sexual mores of the Bible because it felt like putting on a straightjacket. They rejected God's moral code so they could pursue sexual escapades and salaciousness. Calvin called those who embrace the libertine view of ethics as "dead to decency, sunk in the torpor of sin."

Absolute Certainty

Without God, one cannot account for anything. God is the precondition for logic, morality, mathematics, and everything else in the cosmos. This is certain and absolutely true. The truth is simple, and it is powerful.

Absolute morals and logic require God. Only Christianity supplies the necessary *a priori* conditions for logic and moral absolutes. Therefore every time an unbeliever rationally attacks God, he is demonstrating that God lives. Without God, he cannot make any rational assertion. Absolutes are established on God's nature and His law. If someone tries to assert that there are no absolutes, he must use an absolute statement. This is self-impaling. If it is true, it is false. The only absolutes that are not self-refuting are those from God. Anytime nonbelievers assert that something is true universally and immutably, they are wrong if they stand on a non-Christian foundation because their own worldview cannot provide unchanging, universal, and absolute truth.

Absolutes are Absolutely Necessary

If one rejects God, it is impossible for one to supply the preexisting philosophical environment for the invariant, universal, transcendent laws of logic and the immutable, universal, transcendent moral laws. Only an all-knowing, omnipotent, and immutable God can. Hence those who argue against Christianity presuppose it and depend on the preconditions that only Christianity can provide. Absolutes are mandatory and only Christianity can supply the necessary preconditions for absolutes.

I am certain that it is always wrong to rape children and to sexually abuse babies. I am certain because God, who knows all things and holds all power, has revealed it to men. Nuance and relativism cannot cloud-up that clarity. The contrary to ethical absolutes is self-refuting and it is impossible for the God of the Bible not to exist.

The Only Standard

Our means of discerning what is good and right is found in the Bible. It is our authority and guide. Mankind is not the standard. Science cannot be the standard. The Bible alone provides a standard based on an all-knowing and unchanging God. The standard must be based on an unchanging source, or ethics could change. If moral standards could change this would mean: lying and murder on one day are bad. The next day they might be good. This is manifestly impossible and collapses the pedestal it stands on. If lying could be good, there would be no truth, which is a truth claim. This is self-confounding. Honesty is not just important, it must be practiced in order to communicate and live with others.

Jesus alone is the righteous King and He is perfect in holiness. And He gave us righteous law. Jesus as Lawgiver has no competition. He has no match or equivalent. He has no rival. His words transcend all that has been spoken by the lips of man.

Some Diverse Quotes

The only true morality is 'might makes right'. If there isn't a morality decreed by God then logically the strongest should exploit and take advantage of the weak. To be a consistent atheist/evolutionist, one should close down the nursing homes, the schools for the handicapped, and exterminate all the weak. If evolution is true, then humans are just accidental bits of protoplasm. If there is no God, 'might makes right' and you cannot condemn Hitler, Stalin or Mao. They were killing the weak (the least fit of the bits of protoplasm, and doing the human race a favor, if survival of the fittest rules as it does in evolutionism). In the Christian faith, truth makes right, God's truth: Thou shall not murder, thou shall love thy neighbor, turn the other cheek, do good to them that use and abuse you, feed the poor, clothe the naked and love the unlovely.[1]

Since ever man was, he hath too little rejoiced. This only, my brethren, is original sin.[2]

Amiable agnostics will talk cheerfully about "man's search for God." To me, as I then was, they might as well have talked about a mouse's search for the cat.[3]

Every ethical system presupposes, indeed is organically related to, some conception of man's nature and final destiny.[4]

While the atheistic Darwin of the later years cringed under his shawl, suffering an endless catalog of psychosomatic ailments, fearless Christians like Dr. David Livingston and General Charles Gordon roamed Africa to stamp out slave trading... by Arab traders and by the Africans themselves. Livingston, in particular, was a man of such intense Christian conscience that even the Arabs he was struggling to put out of business respected him for his integrity.[5]

Laws are like sausages. It's better not to see them being made.[6]

God-by definition, some would say-cannot be wrong.[7]

The fact that ethics are always an aspect of Christology seems to be little recognized today.[8]

Justice - if we only knew what it was (Socrates).

Moral salvation comes from recovering authentic moral contact with ourselves. Self-determined freedom demands that I break the hold of external impositions and decide for myself.[9]

The legal witness of a woman is equal to half of that of a man. This is because of a deficiency of a woman's mind. Follow camels, and drink their urine for health (commandments of Muhammad).

Do not interfere with the karmaic suffering of the destitute, poor, the afflicted, and the diseased. Their suffering is for their own good... Throw the widow on the funeral pyre of the deceased husband for this is pleasing to Brahma (Hindu laws).

Has Christianity, in fact, stood for a better morality than that of its rivals and opponents? I do not see how any honest student of history can maintain that this is the case.[10]

Don't tell the servants there is no God, or they will steal the silver.[11]

All power grows from the barrel of a gun (Mao Zedong).

Humility is not a virtue... repentance is not a virtue, or in other words, it does not arise from reason, but he who repents of an action is twice as unhappy or as weak as before.[12]

You're thinking in black and white. Think in shades of gray.[13]

Slay the idolaters, wherever you find them, take them captive and besiege them and lie in wait for them and ambush them (Sura 9, Koran).

He may divorce her if she spoils a meal for him (Rabbi Hillel of the Second Temple period).

A man may divorce his wife if he finds a more beautiful woman than she or if she fails to please him (Rabbi Akiva, the Talmud).

It is a divine doctrine which teaches what is right and pleasing unto God and reproves everything that is sin and contrary to God's will. (The Book of Concord).

[When I was an atheist], My argument against God was that the universe seemed so cruel and unjust. But, how had I got this idea of just and unjust? A man does not call a line crooked unless he has some idea of a straight line. What was I comparing this universe with when I called it unjust?[14]

Let us change the rule we have hitherto adopted for the judging what is good. We took our own will as rule; let us now take the will of God.[15]

If there is no God, anything is permitted (Dostoevsky, quoted by R.C. Sproul).[16]

If man is to change ethically, he must be converted.[17]

Think not that I am come to destroy the law, or the prophets; I am not come to destroy, but to fulfill. For verily I say unto you, till heaven and earth pass, one jot or one tittle shall in no way pass from the law, till all is fulfilled (Matthew 5:17-18).

Biblical Law

Oh, how I love your law! I meditate on it all day long (Psalms 119:97).

Everyone who sins breaks the law; in fact, sin is lawlessness (1 John 3:4).

But about the Son He says, "Your throne, O God, will last forever and ever... You have loved righteousness and hated lawlessness" (Hebrews 1:8-9).

We know that the law is good if one uses it properly (1 Timothy 1:8).

What shall we say, then? Is the law sin? Certainly not!... So then, the law is holy, and the commandment is holy, righteous and good... We know that the law is spiritual (Romans 7:7-14).

If you love me, you will keep my commandments. Whoever has my commands and obeys them, he is the one who loves me. He who loves me will be loved by my Father, and I too will love him and show myself to him (John 14:15 & 21).

And this is love: that we walk in obedience to his commands (2 John 6).

Let God be true but every man a liar (Romans 3:4).

Morality

The Cambridge Dictionary of Philosophy defines morality as: "An informal public system applying to all rational persons, governing behavior that affects others, having the lessening of evil or harm as its goal, and including what are commonly known as the moral rules, moral ideals, and moral virtues."[18] The word "ethics" is given the following definition by the same dictionary: "The philosophical study of morality. The word is commonly used interchangeably with morality... and sometimes it is used more narrowly to mean the moral principles of a particular tradition, group, or individual."[19] Theologian Norman Geisler states: "Moral law is morality for conduct... Law is a moral rule by which we are led to act or are withheld from action... God's purpose for law is to regulate human activity."[20]

Many people have fallen for the swindle of the ages, the theory of evolution. This theory, along with Nietzsche's philosophy, has accomplished a lot. What has been accomplished by this chimera, this hoax, this fallacy, this delusion? This theory has given the world's despots and dictators the philosophical and ideological basis for ordering and carrying out the atrocities they had ordered. Stalin, Mao, and the Khmer Rouge butchered over thirty million people in the twentieth century in the name of communism, atheism, and evolution. Evolution not only gives no fundamental basis for morals; it disallows benevolent ethics. The evolutionist's creed is "survival of the fittest." This doctrine hoists the proposition that "might makes right." When one applies this to reality, the strong should take everything they can through force. Under that false worldview, they should go through the country raping, killing and trampling the weak, the handicapped, and the less fortunate. Evolution undermines charitable ethics as it gives men reason to be selfish, inhumane, wicked, murderous, and destructive.

In atheistic evolution, the only thing that is important is promoting the survival of one's own genes to the next generation. Turning the other cheek or doing good to the physically and mentally challenged, only weakens the gene pool, so charity and benevolence should be rejected and the strong should step on anyone they can. I agree with the way Martin Luther King put it in his homily upon receiving his Nobel Peace Prize: "I refuse to believe the notion that man is mere flotsam and jetsam... unable to respond to the eternal oughtness that forever confronts him."

> The statutes of the LORD are right, rejoicing the heart; The commandment of the LORD is pure, enlightening the eyes (Psalms 19:8).

Today, many people assert that there are no moral absolutes. Yet arguing against unchanging moral truths is self-refuting. When one declares that there are no absolute moral laws, he assumes and desires that you take his statement as "true." The word "true" presupposes that there is a true and false, and a right and wrong. What the anti-moralist asserts defeats itself on its own grounds. If he objects to you pointing this out, he also refutes himself. To state that he objects to anything is to assume moral absolutes. Hence, his objection is false and self-nullifying. You ask him, "Do you think that it is 'wrong' to affirm absolutes?" If he answers "No," at that point he has contradicted himself and affirms moral absolutes. If he answers "Yes," you point out that this objection is an absolute moral truth, thus, he refutes himself and assumes the Christian worldview of absolute moral truths.

Universal Binding Laws Presuppose God

> For when Gentiles, who do not have the law, by nature do the things in the law, these, although not having the law, are a law to themselves, who show the work of the law written in their hearts, their conscience also bearing witness, and between themselves their thoughts accusing or else excusing them (Romans 2:14-15).

The moral law was written on the human conscience by nature. This writing has been defaced, but not obliterated. A clear and correct knowledge of the moral law requires the republication of the commandments, summarized in the Decalogue as the permanent and unalterable rule of man's duty on earth.[21]

Without postulating the existence of God it would be impossible to link the moral order to the natural order: the two realms would remain separate. How could the moral laws confront me with the kind of demands they do, how could they come to me with the kind of force they do, unless they have their source in a Being who exists objectively that is, independently of me and is essentially good? ...there is something in every man, it may seem, that demands God as a postulate.[22]

Moral laws are nonmaterial realities that presuppose a nonmaterial God who has the wisdom and authority to decree and enact them. Without God, as the moral lawgiver, there cannot be nonmaterial moral laws. A holy, wise, and good God is the precondition for true, eternal, nonmaterial, and irreducible realities called moral laws. Materialistic atheism cannot account for irreducible nonmaterial entities that are to govern human behavior. Without an omnipotent, sovereign God issuing laws that are based on His perfect character, one has no motivation to obey the law simply because obedience is morally good. Leave God out of the picture and one only obeys the law because of the fear of possible penal sanction and civil punishment from an earthly government. When the civil authorities aren't looking, one can steal, lie, cheat, and rape with impunity. There must be a sovereign God, as the sufficient and universal condition, to obey out of virtue and goodness alone. We have strong motivation to follow laws, when no one is looking, if the laws are intrinsically good, and come from a good, all seeing God - God who commands humanity to love Him by obeying His commandments. When you take away the character and authority of God to enact law, one is not obliged to obey them out of mere virtue and rightness.

Moral Law and The Christian Witness

The moral law is a great tool to help dismantle non-Christian worldviews and lead people to Jesus. Everyone has to acknowledge some form of a moral law (for the few that try to deny moral law see the argument below). The precondition of moral law is the God of the Bible. Here is a sample syllogism to demonstrate that God is inescapable:

1. To postulate that there are no moral absolutes is to make a truth claim.
2. A truth claim presupposes moral absolutes.
3. Hence, there are moral absolutes.
4. Objective moral absolutes can only exist if an immutable, absolute moral Lawgiver exists.
5. Therefore, God, the immutable, absolute moral Lawgiver, exists. It is impossible for Him not to exist.

If one denies the premise, it is impossible for that denial to be true because it would be self-refuting. If that denial were true, one would have the impossible problem of morally demanding that others "ought" to affirm the denial against an absolute moral law. Thus, the denial itself becomes an absolute moral law. If one does not have to affirm the denial absolutely, then it is not universally and absolutely true. Thus it is false. The denial of moral absolutes is self-defeating because the denial of morality presupposes morality. The attempt to deny absolute moral law affirms it. To deny fixed morality is illogical, meaningless, and self-impaling.

There must be an objective absolute Lawgiver. If one tries to fall back on the canard that "all things are meaningless," one commits philosophical suicide. If all things were meaningless, then that would include the statement itself (all things are meaningless). Therefore, it is impossible for all things to be meaningless.

God is Absolutely Required

The only way to avert skepticism is to have an unchanging, infinite, infallible, and exhaustive authority. The God of the Bible alone has these attributes. God is absolutely required because He is unchanging, universal in knowledge, timeless, transcendent, and nonphysical and the laws of logic are unchanging, universal, timeless, transcendent, and nonphysical. Logic is necessary for all assertions, investigations, ethics and evidence; hence God alone provides the necessary preconditions to make sense of our world and experience. The Triune God must exist, the contrary is impossible.

God is the precondition for intellectual certainty. And there must be certainty. The statement that asserts that there is no certainty is self-refuting, because it claims certainty. Hence there must be a certain, immutable, and infallible authority. The only one who can be that authority is God Almighty. All other starting points lack the ability to supply immutability and universals. Christianity is the inescapable truth inasmuch as it alone provides the preconditions for the universal and unchanging laws of logic. Human beings are not omniscient or omnipotent; thus humanity cannot account for the universals in the laws of logic, ethics, and mathematics. Universal and certain claims are unavoidable, and Christianity alone provides the preconditions for universal and certain claims; thus, Christianity must be true.

Without the Triune God, all reasoning fails; thus there could not be science. There is not a non-Christian view of the creation that can make sense out of reasoning, science, and morality. An atheist scientist cannot account for his use of nonphysical logic in his scientific reasoning. Logic is not physical; it is transcendent, universal, and abstract. Only the Christian world and life view can supply the necessary preconditions for the nonmaterial, unchanging, and universal laws of logic. The laws of logic cannot be found in a beaker or a test-tube. You cannot purchase a set of laws of logic on sale at Vons; they are not concrete and physical. Only the transcendent, immutable, universal, and nonphysical God can provide the necessary preconditions for the transcendent, immutable, universal, and nonphysical laws of logic. It is impossible for the atheistic scientist to be correct in declaring that nothing exists except the material. For even that declaration is nonmaterial, therefore it is false. It is impossible for God not to exist.

Polling A Collegiate Relativist

Below I have recorded a conversation between a college student and myself. This is one conversation, out of hundreds, that I have had that fits this pattern. I would encourage the reader to use a similar format when you are sharing your faith with an unbeliever who rejects the notion that there are absolute moral laws.

Mike: Hi, do you have a moment to take a survey?
Frank: What is the subject of the survey?
Mike: I'm collecting opinions on the religious views of the students or lack thereof.
Frank: I'm not religious.
Mike: I will note that in the questionnaire.
Frank: OK.
Mike: Do you have any religious background in your family?
Frank: Yes, my parents are Catholic.
Mike: Do you believe in Jesus?
Frank: I don't know. I believe we all walk our

own path, and you do what feels good to you.

Mike: Do you believe in right and wrong?

Frank: No, I believe that all things are relative. No one has the right to tell me what to do.

Mike: Is it morally wrong to tell you what to do?

Frank: Uh.

Mike: You are caught in a self-refuting statement. All assertions that contradict God's word are in error. You said that no one has the right to tell you what to do. Your statement is a moral law which destroys your assertion that there is no right or wrong.

Frank: Hmm.

Mike: You also must believe that torturing babies and haphazardly storing nuclear waste near Yellowstone National Park are not morally wrong actions.

Frank: Well, uh, no. I didn't say that.

Mike: Yes, you did when you declared that all things are relative and that there is no right and wrong. If it is wrong for you to torture children and destroy the environment, it might not be wrong for someone else to do those things, according to your worldview.

Frank: No way. I believe those things are wrong!

Mike: Then, you do actually believe in right and wrong.

Frank: I guess you're right, but I don't believe in what the Bible says is right and wrong.

Mike: Then what authority do you have that identifies what is good and bad?

Frank: Myself.

Mike: Now you are right back to where you started. If you are the only judge of good and evil, and that judgment is limited to yourself, then you still have the problem of those who believe it is good to exploit and brutalize little children and bring ruin to the environment.

Frank: That's fine, what's your standard?

Mike: The only true standard is God's moral law found in the Bible. It is unchanging, universal, and fixed. God gives mankind a transcendent, immutable moral code that can be applied in all moral choices. Without God, and His objective moral standard, one cannot assert that the Nazi's, slave holders, those who dump nuclear waste in a haphazard way, and mass-murderers are wrong. If moral law is based on individual beliefs, then there is no unchanging moral law. People's beliefs are diverse and change over time. God's law doesn't change and is not ratified as true by the votes of men. It establishes the foundation of righteous civil structure and the principled footing for the ordering of all social relationships. The law cannot change at the whims of men. The moral law is not established on independent, individual beliefs, fickle feelings, convention, or democracy. Morality and justice come from God and His moral law and not mankind's autonomous notions.

Frank: Well, you gave me a lot to think about. Thank you.

Mike: Here is a booklet about God and an invitation to the church I attend.

God and His Law: The Preconditions for Shame

The LORD is compassionate and gracious, slow to anger, abounding in love (Psalms 103:8).

We all feel the emotional state of guilt and shame. This guilt and shame we feel when we break a moral law presupposes God and His fixed just law. A moral obligation can only be justified by appealing to the sovereign, omnipotent, and good Lawgiver. Man feels shame and guilt when he disobeys inasmuch as he has done this to a personal loving God. It is obvious, *prima facie*, that anti-theism is not just to be rejected as a foundation for moral law, but it is impossible. God is the self-existent, holy, and sovereign One who is the foundation of moral law and ethical principles. The beauty of the Christian faith is the truth of God's moral law, and its culminating expression and fulfillment in the gospel. Jesus Christ died on the cross for His children and rose from the dead on the third day. Those, who trust in Jesus, have all their guilt and shame washed away. Yes, God's law presses guilt on our soul, but God is a good and merciful God. Through the cross of Christ, He forgives our sins and gives us forensic (legal) and perfect righteousness in Jesus. Christianity is the only worldview that can account for guilt and shame, and is the only worldview that can remove them. Christianity is the only foundation for moral law and ethics. And it alone provides the remedy for breaking that law through the vicarious atonement of Jesus Christ.

The Eurthyphro Dilemma: A False Dilemma

> God has the right to command, because He is the Source and the End of all things... since man is made in the moral image of God, moral obedience immediately becomes due, from such a creature to his Maker.[23]

The Eurthyphro dilemma asks the question: Is the law morally good because God affirms and loves it, or does God affirm and love it because it is good? These two questions can be asked of the many false gods, but they are not relevant to the true and living God. The first question asks whether a law is good because God says it is good? The question implies: if God says that killing little baby girls in China (to allow more births of boys) is morally right, then it is. A god who has this nature and character cannot be the true and living God, and cannot exist as a good God. Since God is good and His moral law forbids the evil and prescribes the good, He must exist for there to be good moral laws.

The second dilemma is: if God affirms a law because it's good, then there is a ground of goodness that is outside and above God, which He is therein a submissive subject. This means that something would be over God, thus, God is not God. This is impossible. The moral law depends on God because of His many-splendid, perfect character. The moral law is good because a good God decrees and issues them based on His nature and righteous will. Moral law doesn't lie outside God. It comes from His very nature. Therefore, the law is not above God.

The Mafia boss, who establishes iron-fisted control over a neighborhood through brutal force, teaches us that the success of thugs and "wise guys" cannot establish that they are morally right and ethically justified by might alone. The murdering and intimidating of shop owners, and the seizing control over a whole neighborhood is morally evil. Might doesn't make right. The power to impose gangland rule over hard working citizens cannot morally justify the actions of the violent crooks. Thus, God's power cannot justify moral law alone. The moral law is righteous and good because it is grounded on the nature and character of the good and perfect God. The one true God is not subject to moral principles or laws outside Himself. His law is not arbitrary or capricious. He is a perfect and good God who decrees laws and commandments because His being is the source and foundation of all goodness and rightness. All anti-theism, Islam, Buddhism, and Hinduism ultimately deny true moral realism, i.e., that there are real moral laws (commandments that humanity can know and understand). The God of scripture is necessarily good and righteous in His omnipotence and sovereignty. He has the power to decree, issue, and enact moral laws, statutes, and commandments based on His own perfect, immutable nature.

The Self-Refuting Notion of Materialism

Materialism is a physical-only ontology. It asserts the belief that only the physical material universe exists; there are no gods, angels, or spirits. This theory cannot account for or justify nonphysical moral laws. The notion that moral laws do not exist because they are not physical in nature is fallacious. The belief that only the physical world exists cannot even account for itself, since the statement itself is nonphysical. Not only is the statement inadequate, it is self-refuting. If it is true, it is false. Either way, it's not true. Thus it's self-abrogating. If only things that are unfixed, material and divisible exist, then all our nonphysical assertions about that subject do not exist. This is plainly absurd. The ontological basis for discerning right from wrong is nonphysical. God's decree (which all righteous ethics are predicated on) is irrevocably bound to His character and nature. The status and the binding authority of moral laws are not dependent on what men decide. The right to enact laws is not based on the ideas, tastes, judgments, and feelings of mankind.

Pagan Ethics

> Pre-Justinian Roman Law was a collection of inconsistent, and at times, unjust laws that were lax on the treatment of slaves (former and freed slaves), and allowed the rape of women and men within the family, under the husband's almost unbound authority.[24]

Men, who refuse to affirm God's law, base most of their laws on a pragmatic (law is based upon what works best; a moral law is right if it brings about good results) and utilitarian (moral law is right if it produces the most good or utility for the most people; it must provide the greatest amount of happiness for the greatest number of people) approach to ethics. Most legislators enact laws that they hope will do the most good for the most people. They attempt to make laws that are practical and beneficial. To make only those laws that have been calculated to secure public benefit can lead to Nazism, Fascism, and sanctioned kidnapped slavery. The civil law must be based on God's laws and applying the general equity thereof. Universal and immutable law comes from the eternal God who has always been God. If not, law is based on the prejudices, agendas, and the unstable feelings of men. God has written His law on the hearts of all men, yet men suppress His truth in unrighteousness. This is the reason pagan law is inconsistent and it cannot be justified within its own worldview. Only the Christian worldview can give a consistent and righteous moral code. Much of the Justinian legal code, King Alfred's Book of Laws, the Magna Carta, and Blackstone's Commentaries were influenced by the laws, commandments, statutes, and injunctions of scripture. The chief architect of the U.S. Constitution, James Madison, was discipled and taught legal and political ideology by John Witherspoon. Witherspoon was a famous Presbyterian minister and expositor of Holy Writ. He greatly influenced the political theory in the birth of the United States. God's law is the foundation for righteous civil law.

God's Revealed Law

The heavens declare the glory of God; And the firmament shows His handiwork... The law of the LORD is perfect, converting the soul; The testimony of the LORD is sure, making wise the simple; The statutes of the LORD are right, rejoicing the heart; The commandment of the LORD is pure, enlightening the eyes; The fear of the LORD is clean, enduring forever; The judgments of the LORD are true and righteous altogether. More to be desired are they than gold, Yea, than much fine gold; Sweeter also than honey and the honeycomb (Psalms 19:7-10).

For the wrath of God is revealed from heaven against all ungodliness and unrighteousness of men, who suppress the truth in unrighteousness, because what may be known of God is manifest in them, for God has shown it to them. For since the creation of the world His invisible attributes are clearly seen, being understood by the things that are made, even His eternal power and Godhead, so that they are without excuse, because, although they knew God, they did not glorify Him as God, nor were thankful, but became futile in their thoughts, and their foolish hearts were darkened. Professing to be wise, they became fools (Romans 1:18-22).

The Purpose of God's Law

God has revealed His word and His law to mankind. Because of this, we can:

1. Discern, know, and affirm a universal, absolute moral law. Moral laws are unchanging and apply to all persons everywhere always. They are not constructs of social convention and are not subject to human opinion, speculation, culture, social tastes, or personal preferences.

2. Moral laws are revelations (divine communication) of what people "ought" to do. God has clearly revealed, to every person, His moral law.

3. All men, universally, know what they
   should do. God has revealed to our human
   will what we should and should not do.
   This is the reason we have feelings of
   guilt. This worry leads to the stocking of
   the huge selection of titles in the self-help
   sections of major bookstores (they are
   packed with a plethora of self-help titles
   on guilt and shame). Guilt helps spawn
   human religion and all its sacrifices and
   appeasements to nonexistent gods in an
   attempt to remove their guilty feelings.
   Only the Biblical sacrificial system is true.
   It foreshadowed and pictured the effectual
   sacrifice of Jesus Christ on the cross for
   the propitiation of God's wrath, and
   secured the forgiveness of sins for His
   people. Through Christ, the Christian has
   all his guilt and shame removed.

   As a compass directs you through a storm
   at sea, values direct you through the
   challenges of life. Using values to
   determine your next move is simply
   practical.[25]

CHAPTER 2

THE TEN COMMANDMENTS ARE NOT SUGGESTIONS

The Ten Commandments

You shall have no other gods before Me. You shall not make for yourself a carved image, or any likeness of anything that is in heaven above, or that is in the earth beneath, or that is in the water under the earth; you shall not bow down to them nor serve them. For I, the LORD your God, am a jealous God, visiting the iniquity of the fathers on the children to the third and fourth generations of those who hate Me, but showing mercy to thousands, to those who love Me and keep My commandments. You shall not take the name of the LORD your God in vain, for the LORD will not hold him guiltless who takes His name in vain. Remember the Sabbath day, to keep it holy. Six days you shall labor and do all your work, but the seventh day is the Sabbath of the LORD your God. In it you shall do no work: you, nor your son, nor your daughter, nor your male servant, nor your female servant, nor your cattle, nor your stranger who is within your gates. For in six days the LORD made the heavens and the earth, the sea, and all that is in them, and rested the seventh day. Therefore the LORD blessed the Sabbath day and hallowed it. Honor your father and your mother, that your days may be long upon the land which the LORD your God is giving you. You shall not murder. You shall not commit adultery. You shall not steal. You shall not bear false witness against your neighbor. You shall not covet your neighbor's house; you shall not covet your neighbor's wife, nor his male servant, nor his female servant, nor his ox, nor his donkey, nor anything that is your neighbor's. Now all the people witnessed the thunderings, the lightning flashes, the sound of the trumpet, and the mountain smoking; and when the people saw it, they trembled and stood afar off (Exodus 20:1-18).

A man should always learn from the mind of his Maker. Behold the Holy One, blessed be He, ignored mountains and hills and caused His Shechinah to alight Mount Sinai (Talmud).

The only consistent basis for ethics is God's word, the Bible. The Ten Commandments are the foundation for good, just laws and righteous ethical codes. All other systems are inconsistent, and allow evil to intermingle in culture. Muslim societies prohibit freedom and legislate the execution of those who disagree with Islam. In the Muslim nation of Iran, a man got arrested for teaching people to dance. Hinduism, for over two thousand years, legalized the burning of widows in the funeral pyre of their deceased husbands. Charles Spurgeon recounted the story of a Hindu woman that told a missionary: "Surely your Bible was written by a woman." The missionary asked her: "Why do you assert that?" She responded: "Because it says so many kind things about women. Our religion never refers to women except in reproach." The Bible, thousands of years before Western science discovered the problem of microbes and the need to wash and sterilize, commands people to observe strict sanitary guidelines.

The Hindu's consider the Ganges river to be sacred and are commanded to bathe, drink, and swim in its polluted waters. An *Associated Press* release, in the spring of 2002, recounted how the faithful Hindu immerses himself into the Ganges. The result, of this polluted bath, is many of them get skin, intestinal, and stomach ailments from the "holy river." A river that is filled with rotting corpses, ashes of the dead, sewage, and other waste. Many devout Hindus die from the religious rituals of the Ganges that are theologically imposed on the faithful.[26] All religions are not basically the same. All moral codes (whether religious or non-religious) are not the same. Values, morals, and laws that are good and true must come from the Bible. Good morals come from, or are derived from, the general equity of its principles.

The First Commandment:
Have No Other Gods Before God

Many American conservatives are fighting to put the Ten Commandments back in the public schools. It's interesting that many of these people assert that the Ten Commandments are secular. They insist that all people, of all faiths, can affirm them. The truth is the atheist, the Buddhist, the Hindu, and the Muslim, among many other groups, do not believe in the first three commandments. There is no way a practicing Buddhist will throw away his Buddha statues (idols) and go along with those who want to put the Ten Commandments in public places. Without conversion, the Muslim will blow himself up before he will worship the true and living God and forsake Allah. The atheist will run and hug the leg of the ACLU before he will agree with the first three commands. Those who reject Biblical law are in error and should repent and bow down to the one and only Deity, the God of the Bible. But the sham, of proposing that the Ten Commandments are secular in nature, needs to stop. God is God, and the first three commandments demand that full allegiance and worship be given to Him alone. The other seven commandments reflect His nature and are eternally linked with the first three commandments.

The Westminster Shorter Catechism instructs us on the application of the Ten Commandments including the first commandment:

> Q. 39. What is the duty which God requires of man?
> A. The duty which God requires of man is obedience to his revealed will.
>
> Q. 40. What did God at first reveal to man for the rule of his obedience?
> A. The rule which God at first revealed to man for his obedience was the moral law.
>
> Q. 41. Where is the moral law summarily comprehended?
> A. The moral law is summarily comprehended in the ten commandments.
>
> Q. 42. What is the sum of the ten commandments?
> A. The sum of the ten commandments is to love the Lord our God with all our heart, with all our soul, with all our strength, and with all our mind; and our neighbor as ourselves.
>
> Q. 45. Which is the first commandment?
> A. The first commandment is, Thou shall have no other gods before me.
>
> Q. 46. What is required in the first commandment?
> A. The first commandment requires us to know and acknowledge God to be the only true God,

and our God; and to worship and glorify him accordingly.

Q. 47. What is forbidden in the first commandment?
A. The first commandment forbids the denying, or not worshiping and glorifying the true God as God, and our God; and the giving of that worship and glory to any other, which is due to him alone.

Q. 48. What are we specially taught by these words before me in the first commandment?
A. These words before me in the first commandment teach us that God, who sees all things, takes notice of, and is much displeased with, the sin of having any other god.

The God of the Bible is the One and only. There are no other gods in existence, except in the imaginations of men. Thus God has the authority to require all men, in all ages, in all places, to honor Him alone. It is humorous to watch the conservative talking heads on TV declare that the Ten Commandments are not religious. The laughing ends when they declare that the Decalogue is the foundation for secular society. They often stress that the Ten Commandments are valuable solely for pragmatic and cultural reasons. Every time I hear a pundit proclaim such nonsense, I always wonder if they have ever read them. The first commandment enjoins all people to put away all false gods, whether that is Allah, Krishna, Shiva, the Mormon deity, or any other false god. The literal injunction is to have no other gods before God's face. He sees everything. And He flat out commands all men to dispel other deities from their heart, life, and worship. All claims from other gods are just the profane and ridiculous ideas of men. The first commandment is the most sacred of all the commandments: we are bound to affirm and profess that there is but one God only; the Most High, and to honor and worship Him alone.

The Second Commandment: Do Away with All Idols

The second commandment forbids the making, having, affirming, and bowing down to an idol. If a person has an idol, he will also be led to break some of the other nine commandments. God is a jealous God, and He "shows mercy unto thousands... who love me and keep my commandments." Note: the English word "commandments" is a translation of the Hebrew word *Mitzvah*. This word binds people to all His commandments. The Hebrew word that means "to hew and to shape" is *pasal*. This means to carve or shape an object into the likeness of an animal, man, plant, or some other entity. The injunction forbids the production of anything, in any likeness, to be used as an object of worship.

Modern Idols

Our culture has erected a plethora of idols in sports and entertainment. Rock stars and movie stars are *idolized* by masses. We have teen idols and sports idols. Fans of Michael Jordan would wave placards declaring that Jordan was God. Yikes! Southern California Heisman trophy winner Matt Leinart became more than the big man on campus after he led the Trojans to the National title in college football. His college campus ordained laws that went over the top. One rule regulated the proper way one must speak of him: It had to be Matt Leinart. It could never be plain Matt or plain Leinart, but he was to always be spoken of as Matt Leinart. One student saw Leinart and almost fainted at just a quick glance. His superstar status resulted in news reports of every move he made during routine days as a student: "Matt Leinart dropped a pen today. And then he picked it up!" Esteeming mere men in an exaggerated manner is idolatry. It is rampant in our world and should be repudiated and shunned by all.

Many religious people take the second commandment as a prohibition of all art, objects molded into a likeness of any living being, even toy dolls for children. Yet the prohibition is against bowing down to them or worshiping them. Therefore we are instructed to worship God in "Spirit and in truth" not through man made objects. Philo wisely stated, "Let no one... of those beings who are endowed with souls, worship anything that is devoid of a soul." We must do away with all idols of the mind and the earth.

The Catechism continues its instruction with the second commandment:

> Q. 49. Which is the second commandment?
> A. The second commandment is, Thou shall not make unto thee any graven image, or any likeness of anything that is in heaven above, or that is in the earth beneath, or that is in the water under the earth: thou shall not bow down thyself to them, nor serve them: for I the Lord thy God am a jealous God, visiting the iniquity of the fathers upon the children unto the third and fourth generation of them that hate me; and showing mercy unto thousands of them that love me, and keep my commandments.
>
> Q. 50. What is required in the second commandment?
> A. The second commandment requires the receiving, observing, and keeping pure and entire, all such religious worship and ordinances as God hath appointed in his word.
>
> Q. 51. What is forbidden in the second commandment?
> A. The second commandment forbids the

worshiping of God by images, or any other way
not appointed in his word.

Q. 52. What are the reasons annexed to the second
commandment?
A. The reasons annexed to the second
commandment are, God's sovereignty over us, his
propriety in us, and the zeal he hath to his own
worship.

The Third Commandment: Honoring God's Name

We are not just to put away idolatry, but we should have a
passion to uphold God's honor and His name. John Calvin, the
great theologian and reformer (he was the theological father of the
Pilgrims and the Puritans, thus he is called the philosophical
grandfather of the American Government), brilliantly taught:

> "[that] if we had one grain of intelligence, we
> would be zealous for the honor of God, so much
> so that it would be entirely unnecessary for
> anyone to solicit us to that end. We should be
> engaged in fulfilling what is written in the Psalms:
> that this zeal should devour us, that we should be
> engulfed by it; and should we see anyone casting
> opprobrium against His majesty, or vilifying it, of
> necessity we would feel a burning fire within us.
> But observe! We are so careful to maintain our
> own honor, yet whenever the world abandons
> itself into idolatry, we allow the honor of God to
> be trampled under foot..."[27]

The third commandment is broken in almost every recent
Hollywood movie. It is almost impossible to watch a modern
movie without the actors seemingly insisting that God's last name

29

is damn. It is not. The movie industry also pushes the use of Jesus' name as a cuss word. It is employed, by the uneducated, to express themselves more forcefully. You never hear anyone say, "Oh Muhammad!" or "Oh Buddha!" or "Oh Krishna!" You will never hear anyone curse any false god. It is always God or Jesus. Those names are used as a swear word and used in vain. Even the Christian President, George W. Bush, when he was irritated that a phone message was not heard due to a technical problem, reacted by bemoaning, "G–D dang it!"[28] I have also heard numerous average Christians use the name of God in vain. It is a major problem and reflects the breakdown of American morals, inside and outside the church.

The injunction to not take the Lord's name in vain requires mankind to respect and honor His holy name. The English word "vain" is the translation of the Hebrew word *shavah*, which means: useless, vanity, emptiness, or nothingness. The command is to never blaspheme, utter, declare, speak, or use God's name in a disrespectful, idle, or an empty manner. Our duty is to respect *Ha Shem* (the name) and to never treat it lightly. Jesus at the start of the Lord's Prayer says, "Our Father... hallowed be Thy name." To hallow is to esteem as holy and to honor and revere His name.

The catechism nicely sums up the third commandment:

> Q. 53. Which is the third commandment?
> A. The third commandment is, Thou shall not take the name of the Lord thy God in vain: for the Lord will not hold him guiltless that takes his name in vain.

> Q. 54. What is required in the third commandment?
> A. The third commandment requires the holy and reverent use of God's names, titles, attributes, ordinances, word and works.

Q. 55. What is forbidden in the third commandment?
A. The third commandment forbids all profaning or abusing of anything whereby God makes himself known.

Q. 56. What is the reason annexed to the third commandment?
A. The reason annexed to the third commandment is that however the breakers of this commandment may escape punishment from men, yet the Lord our God will not suffer them to escape his righteous judgment.

The Fourth Commandment:
Every Seventh Day is a Holiday

The fourth commandment requires a day of rest and worship: the worship of the true God. It is not just a day to mow the lawn, wash the car, nap and drink lemonade. It is the Lord's Day. It is a day to put away work and the cares of our earthly vocation. We rest in God and His truth as we spend the day in worship and honoring Him. Modern science has discovered, those who rest once a week and go to Church, live longer than those who neglect church attendance. Many scientific studies have discovered that consistent church attendees are mentally and physically healthier, have less stress, and less heart disease, than those who do not go to church. A great body of research has found that the more faithful and more often one goes to church, the greater the health benefits. The Lord blessed the day, and those who keep it receive multiplied blessings. But we are not to observe the Lord's Day just to gain benefits and blessings. We honor God on this day because He is God, and He is worthy of honor and glory.

The catechism teaches us the delight of the Lord's Day is in the fourth commandment:

Q. 57. Which is the fourth commandment?
A. The fourth commandment is, Remember the Sabbath day, to keep it holy. Six days shall thou labor, and do all thy work: but the seventh day is the Sabbath of the Lord thy God: in it thou shall not do any work, thou, nor thy son, nor thy daughter, thy manservant, nor thy maidservant, nor thy cattle, nor thy stranger that is within thy gates: for in six days the Lord made heaven and earth, the sea, and all that in them is, and rested the seventh day: wherefore the Lord blessed the Sabbath day, and hallowed it.

Q. 58. What is required in the fourth commandment?
A. The fourth commandment requires the keeping holy to God such set times as he hath appointed in his word; expressly one whole day in seven, to be a holy Sabbath to himself.

The Fifth Commandment:
Honoring God-given Authority in the Home

The fifth commandment is listed before the prohibition of murder in the second table of the Decalogue. This demonstrates how important honoring our parents must be. Much of American culture doesn't practice this and they choose to dishonor their mother and father. In fact, much of the culture celebrates the disrespecting of parents. Ozzie Osborne's family had a hit TV show on cable in 2003. It was a smash hit. Part of the reason for its success was that Ozzie's kids cussed him out. This should be an outrage in our country. We surely have fallen a long way from Ozzie and Harriet to Ozzie Osborne. It is evil to disrespect one's parents. It is good to honor your father and mother. It is evil to dishonor them. This is the heart of the Ten Commandments that targets human to human relations. The atheist cannot give a reason we ought to honor our parents. If natural selection is true, then life is like a *Mad Max* movie. It becomes the survival of the fittest. If mom and dad get in my way, then they are my next meal. Consistent atheism cannot supply an objective reason to respect my mother and father. The word "honor" is translated from the Hebrew word *kaved* and is defined as: to honor; make honorable; esteem as worthy; to glorify. In the Biblical worldview, the family is the foundation for a righteous and prosperous society. The child is responsible to the parents and must respect their authority if the social structure is to remain strong. If one doesn't honor one's parents and their authority, they will not honor ecclesiastical or civil authority. The Christian worldview supplies the answer to all the problems in culture and civil society. God's moral laws that enjoin the family are for the wholeness of the family and civilization.

The Catechism sums up our duty to authority:

Q. 63. Which is the fifth commandment?
A. The fifth commandment is, Honor thy father and thy mother; that thy days may be long upon the land which the Lord thy God gives thee.

Q. 64. What is required in the fifth commandment?
A. The fifth commandment requires the preserving the honor, and performing the duties, belonging to every one in their several places and relations, as superiors, inferiors or equals.

Q. 65. What is forbidden in the fifth commandment?
A. The fifth commandment forbids the neglecting of, or doing anything against, the honor and duty that belongs to every one in their several places and relations.

Q. 66. What is the reason annexed to the fifth commandment?

A. The reason annexed to the fifth commandment is a promise of long life and prosperity (as far as it shall serve for God's glory and their own good) to all such as keep this commandment.

The Sixth Commandment: Prohibition of Murder

The translation of the sixth commandment: "You shall not kill," is a mistranslation. The best and clearest translation is: You shall not murder. The injunction is against the premeditated assassination of the innocent. Killing a disease-carrying fly is not forbidden in this law, nor is killing another human being in self-defense. The Hebrew word used for murder (killing) is *ratzach*. This means: to murder; assassinate; slay another with premeditation. The Bible gives allowances for justifiable homicide in war, killing in self-defense, and in the execution of criminals who have committed capitol crimes. An eye for an eye: if you take a life unlawfully, the state will judicially try you and if found guilty, take your life. Individuals should forgive all crimes against them, but the state is to administer justice and execute murderers. God's law enjoins the state to take the life of those who willingly murder innocent men and women.

The catechism on the commandment that forbids unlawful killing:

Q. 67. Which is the sixth commandment?

A. The sixth commandment is, Thou shall not kill.

Q. 68. What is required in the sixth commandment?

A. The sixth commandment requires all lawful endeavors to preserve our own life, and the life of others.

Q. 69. What is forbidden in the sixth
commandment?
A. The sixth commandment forbids the taking
away of our own life, or the life of our neighbor
unjustly, or whatsoever tends thereunto.

The Seventh Commandment:
A Code for Sexual Purity

Most modern defenders of sexual purity use pragmatism to
preach against extramarital affairs and fornication. They assert
that if one behaves in an immoral manner sexually, one will more
likely endure harmful repercussions. Most of the "Abstinence-
only programs teach adolescents that 'sexual activity outside the
context of marriage is likely to have harmful psychological and
physical effects'... comprehensive programs... mention the
benefits of abstinence... When we talk about smoking we teach
kids not to do it, period; we don't teach them how to choose
brands that are low in tar and nicotine."[29] The only time in the
American media that you hear that fornication is morally wrong is
from the mouths of religious people. Frequently, even many
churchmen give mostly pragmatic reasons to prohibit sexual
immorality. Obviously, there are hundreds of studies that
demonstrate that living a sexually immoral life results in a higher
rate of infections, disease, mental and physical illness, and a
shorter life span. Yet, the main reason we declare that adultery
and fornication are morally wrong is: God has declared that
sexual immorality is wrong based on His holy character.

The Seventh Commandment according to the catechism
instruction is:

Q. 70. Which is the seventh commandment?
A. The seventh commandment is, Thou shall not
commit adultery.

Q. 71. What is required in the seventh commandment?
A. The seventh commandment requires the preservation of our own and our neighbor's chastity, in heart, speech and behavior.

Q. 72. What is forbidden in the seventh commandment?
A. The seventh commandment forbids all unchaste thoughts, words and actions.

The Eighth Commandment:
Property Rights are God Given

The reason kids shouldn't steal is because it's wrong. Period. It's right there in the Ten Commandments... All our laws descend originally from those tablets handed down by Moses... Yet, we can't publicly tell kids in our society to obey these laws because they have a religious origin. We dare not suggest to them that there is a higher morality than our state and national laws. We can't introduce the idea that they will have to answer to God for their behavior. Let me tell you, folks, you don't want to live in a society in which the great majority of the people do not believe ultimately they are accountable to an authority higher than the state. That is a recipe for national disaster.[30]

The eighth commandment forbids one to steal. The Biblical word in Hebrew for the English word "steal" is *ganav*. This word means to grab or take by stealth. Hence this commandment prohibits the seizing, robbing, plundering, and pillaging of another person's property no matter how small or large. Stealing is closely linked to lying because the Hebrew word is linked to deception. The ground for individual property rights comes from this verse. We take it for granted that my house is my house, and I own all the things inside it. Yet many cultures throughout history did not recognize personal property rights. The American government and other nations affirmed property rights because of Christianity and its prohibitions against stealing.

Since stealing is rooted and linked to deception, the application of this law requires CEO's and other corporate heads to be honest and righteous in their business dealings with their stock holders and the public. In the summer of 2002, we saw a wave of corporate misdealing and malfeasance. This is an outrage because God has said you shall not stealthily "steal."

The catechism teaches that the commandment not to steal requires:

Q. 73. Which is the eighth commandment?
A. The eighth commandment is, Thou shall not steal.

Q. 74. What is required in the eighth commandment?
A. The eighth commandment requires the lawful procuring and furthering the wealth and outward estate of ourselves and others.

Q. 75. What is forbidden in the eighth commandment?
A. The eighth commandment forbids whatsoever does or may unjustly hinder our own or our neighbor's wealth or outward estate.

The Ninth Commandment:
The Requirement to Tell the Truth

Lying lips are an abomination to the LORD, but those who deal truthfully are His delight (Proverbs 12:22).

"The ninth commandment is a prohibition against deception, lying, and bearing false witness. It also forbids speaking that which is false. It has application for education, science, relationships, civil justice, and sports. In sports, games have rules that you must obey. The referee or the umpire should not lie about a ball going out of bounds or in the strike zone. If the referee is untruthful, the game is unfair and loses its appeal. Athletic games presuppose the moral Lawgiver."[31] Without God, one cannot justify rules for sports and games.

Columnist Jane Eisner of *Knight Ridder Newspapers* engages lying head-on:

"Lying is a no-no. The liar says hello to the truth, shakes its hand, then deliberately flips it inside out and stomps it to the ground. Lying damages the social bonds that knit together a culture because it destroys trust; surely that's why bearing false witness is up there with murder and adultery as the great prohibitions in Biblical law. And of course, lying gets you into trouble."

Science also presupposes God, the moral Lawgiver, and the ninth commandment inasmuch as it is wrong for a scientist to be untruthful and dishonest with his data. If most scientists were to falsify data, in their medical research on cancer or heart disease, the result would be a huge loss of life. Therefore good science depends on God.

Cheating on tests at college is immoral. If there were numerous college cheats, after graduation they would be released in society without the proper training they need to perform their vocation competently. Many people could be injured, hurt, or killed by the mistakes of the improperly trained employees. We should be truthful people. All the structures and foundations of civil society rely on the majority of the people keeping this law. Serial cultural dishonesty would lead to the collapse of peaceful civil society. God's ninth commandment reflects His righteousness and protects all society. We are to affirm and embrace this commandment everyday, in every way.

The catechism continues by instructing us on the requirement of the ninth commandment:

> Q. 76. Which is the ninth commandment?
> A. The ninth commandment is, Thou shall not bear false witness against thy neighbor.

> Q. 77. What is required in the ninth commandment?
> A. The ninth commandment requires the maintaining and promoting of truth between man and man, and of our own and our neighbor's good name, especially in witness-bearing.

> Q. 78. What is forbidden in the ninth commandment?
> A. The ninth commandment forbids whatsoever is prejudicial to truth, or injurious to our own or our neighbor's good name.

Without a prescription from a transcendent holy God, one can lie and label cruelty as non-cruelty; murder as non-murder, stealing as non-stealing and on and on. This brings to light the connection between the laws of logic and ethics. Logic presupposes telling the truth. If not, one can assert that "A" is "non-A." Without logic and the prohibition against lying, everything is the same, one cannot make a distinction. One must make distinctions to account for anything, including morality and logic. Hence, ethics, including the prohibition against lying, are necessary *a priori* conditions for all human experiences. Human experiences requires us to make accurate distinctions. It is self-stultifying to deny the necessity of truth telling: one would only have to repeat any sentence back to the denier as the opposite, including truth telling is not necessary. To the one who asserts that, just tell them that they in fact said that truth telling IS necessary. They should quickly see the problem. Truth telling is a requirement for intelligible communication.

The Tenth Commandment:
The Forgotten Law Prohibiting Ungodly Desire

The final command is an injunction against coveting. It forbids men to have an unhealthy, idolatrous, or selfish attitude towards other things or other people. To "desire more than is enough" is how Augustine put it. We are not to be consumed with an unbalanced obsessive passion for things that do not belong to us. This commandment is the one most forgotten in American culture. The media fills us with commercials aimed at "consumers." These ads are produced by highly paid and highly skilled men and women who aim to entice us into buying their product. We are bombarded by the advertising media trying to seduce us into coveting their product. Coveting leads to complaining since we think that we do not have a big enough house, with nice enough stuff, hauled by a jazzy enough car. This insatiable appetite can drive us into a love of money. The Bible teaches that the "love of money is the root of all kinds of evil." Covetousness leads to a hyper-desire for money so we can purchase more, bigger, and better stuff. The prohibition against coveting is a law that has its main application on the individual heart. We are to pray and fight, with all our might, to restrain the coveting impulses. These passions can rise up and dominate our moods, relationships, and life. Contentment is a godly attitude and we must cultivate this daily through God's word and His Spirit.

The Catechism teaches us our duty in obeying the tenth commandment is the following:

> Q. 79. Which is the tenth commandment?
> A. The tenth commandment is, Thou shall not covet thy neighbor's house, thou shall not covet thy neighbor's wife, nor his manservant, nor his maidservant, nor his ox, nor his ass, nor anything that is thy neighbor's.
>
> Q. 80. What is required in the tenth commandment?
> A. The tenth commandment requires full contentment with our own condition, with a right and charitable frame of spirit toward our neighbor, and all that is his.
>
> Q. 81. What is forbidden in the tenth commandment?
> A. The tenth commandment forbids all discontentment with our own estate, envying or grieving at the good of our neighbor, and all inordinate motions and affections to anything that is his.
> Q. 82. Is any man able perfectly to keep the commandments of God?
> A. No mere man since the fall is able in this life perfectly to keep the commandments of God, but does daily break them in thought, word and deed.

The Ten Commandments are binding to all people. Yet there is a major breakdown of these laws in Western culture. 74 percent of people polled will steal in given situations; 64 percent will drink and drive; and over 60 percent admit that they would commit adultery in certain circumstances. This is a sad commentary on the attitude of the average American. The Christian and all American citizens must know the Ten Commandments and follow them. If not, our nation is doomed.

CHAPTER 3
THE REALITY OF GOOD AND EVIL

C.S. Lewis taught, one of "evil's shrewdest tricks" is to try to convince humanity that it doesn't exist. Recently, there has been a return to the use of the words "good and evil." President George W. Bush invoked these words in describing the war against terrorism. Those that would massacre civilians, declared Bush, are "evil doers." And President Bush is correct in this judgment. In times of peace and prosperity, it is easy to lie back in the sun and assert that there are no absolute moral laws, all is relative, and there is no right or wrong. When war or some other horror comes upon a nation, most people quickly put their relativistic claims back in their closet. In the first few days after 9/11 very few people came out and tried to refute President Bush for calling Bin Laden and his cronies evil.

Albert Camus (spoken before he converted to Christianity: www.religion-online.org/showarticle) was very troubled about Nazism. He, as an atheist, asserted that all is meaningless, life is absurd, and that nothing really matters. But in the face of the Nazi atrocities, he was deeply troubled and perplexed. He wondered how he could call Nazism wrong if everything is meaningless and absurd? These questions seemed to haunt him until late in life, when he turned and trusted in Jesus Christ.

The Problem of Evil

> Katrina...seemed more like an example of malicious design (Robert Mc Clory on the problem that Hurricane Katrina presents to the Intelligent Design movement).

> It is the best gift God has given men... but for it we could not tell right from wrong (Abraham Lincoln speaking of the Holy Bible).

All men know that evil exists. History posits, page after page, the wicked actions of men toward other men. Racism, genocide, holocaust, terrorism, abortion, persecution, and innumerable acts of inhumanity against humanity are recorded in the history books of mankind. Disease and pain are also difficult elements within the problem of evil. C.S. Lewis wrote a wonderful book on this subject titled *The Problem of Pain*. In that book, he demonstrates that the Christian faith is the only ideology that can truly call evil, evil. If you reject the triune God, you cannot account for evil. In order to claim there is evil, you must presuppose a good law, and to do so requires a good Lawgiver who has revealed His law to mankind. If you deny God because of the existence of evil, you lose the ability to declare that anything is evil. Without God and His law, you cannot distinguish between good and evil, right and wrong. When someone professes that there is no right or wrong, all you have to do is ask them if that statement is right or wrong? No matter how they answer the question, they are caught in a pickle. Those who deny that there is right and wrong, contradict themselves in the very statement they are proclaiming. When you try to eliminate God and His law, you give up the ability to declare anything evil. Evil can only be accounted as evil, if God has revealed an objective and unchanging moral law.

Evil Presupposes Good

The argument: If God is all good and all powerful, He would defeat evil; evil exists, thus God does not exist. This is a fallacious argument and this argument presupposes God. The argument itself depends on God's existence. Even an argument against God's existence, depends upon the preconditions that only the Lord can supply. The argument attempts to disprove God's existence utilizing logic, morality, and a distinction between good and evil. God is the required precondition for the laws of logic and fixed morality. He is the basis for making a distinction between good and evil. Without God, everything just is. There can be no objective moral truths. There can be no truths. When a man asserts good and evil, he presupposes that the triune God lives.

Many atheists frame the argument of evil like this:

1. *If God is all good and all powerful He would defeat evil.*
2. *Evil is not defeated.*
3. *Therefore God does not exist.*

The transcendental argument demonstrates that this argument presupposes God. But the syllogism itself is not even valid. A Christian should never accept the syllogism as it is written above. The way we should pose the formula is this:

1. *If God is all good and all powerful, He can defeat evil.*
2. *Evil is not yet defeated.*
3. *Therefore, God will defeat evil in the future.*

The Bible testifies that one day, God will rinse the world of evil. Evil will be defeated. When one makes an argument, one has God as the ultimate ground for the logic that is employed in the argument, including an argument from evil. The Christian is to examine the argument, and only accept it if it is consistent with the teaching of scripture. The atheist has no way of knowing that in the future God will not defeat evil. The believer has God's word on it. The atheist is left holding an empty bag, a bag that God made. The grounds, from which an atheist attacks God, are based on God's revelation. The atheist has to borrow from the Christian worldview to attempt to disprove God. Only in the context of the Christian worldview is good and evil intelligible. The existence of God is well beyond just a reasonable proof. God is the foundation for knowing anything at all. Deny God, and a man cannot make sense out of anything, including good and evil.

Give Answers with Meekness and Respect

We must never respond to questions about evil in a nonchalant, callous or detached way. We must have compassion for those who struggle with this paradox. Many of those, who focus on this question, have lost loved ones through criminal actions, disease, or natural disasters. A post September eleventh Barna survey found:

> Those who believe in an all-powerful, all knowing God dropped from 72 percent pre-attack to 68 percent afterward.

> Confidence in absolute moral truths dropped from 38 percent to 22 percent.

People are emotional. Both lost people and saved people live on emotions. We are instructed by scripture to be ready to give a defense of our hope with meekness, gentleness, and respect. Truth can transform, and it is beautiful. Love rejoices in the truth, but truth is more than this. Truth is fully true, and it is not false. There are real and true things that are objectively true - regardless whether we like them or not. We should stand for the truth, but with the understanding that our witness is not just an academic debate. There are real, hard hitting, and unpleasant issues we must tackle with love and humility. We must care. I pray over and over that I would care for people. I ask God to give me compassion. Jesus' ministry was known for its compassionate thrust. Truth should always be enjoined with love and humility. Often, people will have stern intellectual problems with Christianity, yet, when you answer them with love and truth, they will melt and almost break down in tears. Jesus wants His followers to touch minds and hearts. The Holy Spirit is the comforter. He comes when we minister to the lost, and He touches them in the depth of their souls. The individual's problem with evil is usually a spiritual and emotional problem more than an intellectual one.

The Christian doesn't have a complete and full understanding of the solution to the problem of evil. Yet Christianity alone can account for the reality of evil, and the future elimination of all evil. God has a holy and righteous reason for the existence of evil, and He has chosen not to reveal it to mankind. Christianity is the only worldview that can objectively identify evil and good. The whole world knows that there is evil in the world. Many of the Eastern religions call it an illusion, but they cannot live consistently with that profession. If a Hindu or a Buddhist asserts that everything is just an illusion; ask him, why does he look both ways before he crosses the street? He shouldn't avoid getting hit by a truck. The truck hitting him is only an illusion according to his worldview. If anything, he should embrace the crash. Getting whacked and smashed into the pavement only hastens his goal of becoming "one with the universe." This is absurd and one of the many reasons the Eastern worldview is false and dangerous. All people know that evil exists, and that right and wrong presuppose God. Even a subject, as difficult as the existence of evil, must assume God to objectively assert that evil exists.

MICHAEL A ROBINSON

The Non-Christian Cannot Account for Good

The anti-theist doesn't have an answer to the problem of evil, nor does he have an answer to the "problem of good." The Christian can justify calling something good, but the anti-theist cannot. Thus he has what has been referred to as "the problem of good." Why is there good in the world? How can you account for that good? By what standard can you call something good? The non-theist's problem of good, presupposes an objective standard of good and evil. Good and evil can only exist if God, the absolute moral agent, has decreed a moral code based on His character. Augustine correctly asks: "If there is no God, why is there so much good?" History informs us that Christians were the first to build institutionalized hospitals, orphanages, and shelters. They did this because it was good, according to the standard of the Bible. The law of Christ was the ideology that led Christians to oppose and help overturn slavery in Western Europe and in America. If anti-theism were true, the outplay of that ideology would be gang rape, torture, and genocide inasmuch as a human would not have any more value than a gnat or a mouse. The obstinate Ted Turner may call Christians "Bozo's," and assert that the Ten Commandments were "obsolete," but without God it is impossible to have an unchanging standard for moral codes.

Autonomous reason cannot justify or establish a set of universal, immutable moral codes. Hitler's "reason," as the ground for moral codes, is different than Martin Luther King's "reason." The Islamic homicide bomber's "reason" is different than Mother Teresa's "reason" as the ground for moral codes. Socrates and other philosophers can claim that man's unaided reason can establish the ground for moral absolutes, but they cannot justify that assertion. There is no universal "reason" that all men agree upon. Ghengis Khan, Stalin, Mao, Lincoln, Jefferson, Billy Graham, and the Ayatollahs have a wide gulf between themselves on what "reason" dictates as right or wrong. The atheistic naturalist cannot find the ground, through reason for an absolute, universal moral code. They claim that the "brain

48

secretes thoughts like the liver secretes bile." We have no reason to trust or obey our "reason." Frame posits: "People get enraged and often outraged at the sight of holocausts, slavery, spouse abuse, rape, and mass murder. We believe that it is not only appropriate to have righteous anger, but people who are cruel have done what they ought not have done. They have violated objective rules that are everywhere in force."[32] We know that rape and slavery are wrong, not because these are preferable over kindness, like a cheeseburger is over a plain burger. It is wrong because it is evil. A just moral code must come from an immutable, universal, and objective moral agent: God Almighty. God is the absolute precondition for objective moral codes.

Moral Relativism is Self-Defeating

Moral relativism is unworkable, self-refuting, but above all else, it is wrong. There are moral absolutes inasmuch as they are founded upon the nature of an absolute, unchanging, and righteous God. The inability of the materialistic atheist, to account for the nonmaterial laws of morality, demonstrates the necessity of God the Lawgiver. Those who cling to materialism, or any other non-Christian worldview, cannot account for unchanging moral laws. This logical problem is a difficulty we are to imprint on them, over and over. This is the reason for my employment of the redundant truth that all non-Christian worldviews cannot justify absolute moral codes. I have repeated this warranted argument, paragraph after paragraph, in the hope that this repetition will make it easier to learn and use in witnessing. Those who reject God also reject absolute moral laws. This is a major philosophical dilemma for the relativist because all men affirm some type of a universal ethical code. The rational and empirical analysis of scientific observations cannot justify ethics. Data cannot provide the "ought" to a worldview. One has to go to a transcendent moral law from the mind of a transcendent Lawgiver, God, to justify the "ought." Without God, there is no ultimate and immutable basis for moral laws. Yet no one can live or communicate without moral laws.

> Before the mountains were brought forth You had formed the earth...from everlasting to everlasting, You are God (Psalms 90:2).

Nazi genocide is wrong. All rape is wrong. Child abuse is wrong. These heinous actions are universally wrong. These are evil acts. Individuals and society are bound to right ethics by God. Righteous laws are good in and of themselves because they come from a good God. The God inspired moral code outlines the duties of mankind. It's not just an axiomatic system, nor is it true and binding inasmuch as they are self-evident truths, first principles, or discerned by pure reason. They are absolute because they reflect the nature of God's divine being. Our conduct is to be regulated by the law that comes to man by the authority derivative from a good and immutable God. A moral relativist cannot declare that anything is right or wrong within his worldview. All non-Christian worldviews ultimately lead to the denial of unchanging ethical laws. Moral absolutes are true and must not be violated. God alone is the one who makes unchanging moral standards true. Moral absolutes not only point to God, but without God, no one can have any moral absolutes. This is self-defeating, thus God must exist.

People declare that all things are relative out of one side of their mouth, then defend environmentalism as if it is always true out of the other side of their mouth. They know that relativism is not true! Obviously, relativism is a self-voiding notion, but they just do not want to be tough-minded and think through life's important issues. Thus many throw around relativistic canards without ever thinking critically about the ground of their claims.

Unjustified Opinions

Pronounce them guilty, O God; let them fall by their own counsels; cast them out in the multitude of their transgressions; for they have rebelled against You (Psalms 5:10).

If you throw around the slogan, "All things are relative," I will ask you whether mistreating slaves is wrong, or murdering homosexuals is wrong, or dumping nuclear waste in the ocean is wrong? Almost every relativist will agree that those things are wrong. Christians can objectively decry the mistreatment of humans and the environment, because we know that God told us not to abuse people and nature. Those who deny absolute truth and values cannot live consistently within the boundaries of that philosophy. No one can consistently live out a life based on relativism. They will stand for something: Human rights, the right to vote, or something that is of great value to them. Once they assert that something should be done or not done, they have borrowed from the Christian worldview. No other worldview can give an unchanging, perpetual, universal, and absolute standard for ethics and morality. All systems of ethics and science will ultimately be relativistic except for Christianity. The Christian ethical law is based on the eternal, unchanging, and absolute nature of God. All other systems are based on opinion, the opinion of the masses or men of letters. Either way, it is their opinion, and opinions change. There are some absolutes, some things that are immutably true, some things that are not subject to opinion.

Absolutes are established on God's nature and His law. If someone tries to assert that there are no absolutes, he must use an absolute statement. This, as we have now learned, is self-impaling. If it is true, it is false. The only absolutes that are not self-refuting are those from God. So anytime relativists assert that something is true universally and immutably, they are wrong if they stand on a non-Christian foundation because their own worldview cannot provide unchanging, universal, and absolute truth; that is devastating, and the truth found in Christ devastates and demolishes all vain imaginations.

> Casting down arguments, and every high thing that exalts itself against the knowledge of God, bringing every thought into captivity to the obedience of Christ (2 Corinthians 10:4-5).

Liars and Truth

> Jesus said to him, "I am the way, the truth, and the life..." (John 14:6).

> In the matter of just and unjust, fair and foul, good and evil, which are the subjects of our present consultation, ought we follow the opinion of many and to fear them; or the opinion of the many who has understanding? (Plato quoting Socrates).

> Let God be true, and every man a liar... (Romans 3:4).

To have a consistent and functional worldview, one must have absolute standards and laws. If one asserts laws that do not come from God's revealed word, these assertions will be self-contradictory and self-defeating. When the non-Christian claims that there are no absolutes, he is asserting an absolute standard and a law, a standard that is self-stultifying. The statement that there are no absolutes is an absolute statement. This statement is a contradiction and self-refuting; for it to be true, it would have to be false; therefore, it can only be false. There must be absolutes in logic and in morality, or we can assert nothing and account for nothing; that is impossible.

Unchanging standards do not reside in matter and cannot be

empirically quantified, examined, or put into a flask. They cannot be human conventions or subjective theories made up by mutable man. The absolutes of ethics transcend time, space, and matter and cannot be tested in a lab. But all labs assume absolutes and use them in all their science. They cannot solely be the result of neuron firings in the brain, because that would make them mutable, and by definition they would not be laws. The material-only atheist cannot explain from where laws come or justify them anymore than frontal lobe challenged boxer Riddock Bowe. It was Bowe, reported in the *Las Vegas Review Journal*, who kidnapped his wife because he "wasn't thinking correctly." This "mistaken attempt to get his family together" was blamed on frontal lobe damage from years of boxing. He later admitted that his lawyers cooked-up the idea to try to keep him out of jail. Much of our legal system is based on relativism and not the pursuit of truth. Thus, Bowe and his lawyers never even blushed in their admission of this fraudulent defense. The notion of morals without absolutes must be rinsed out of our culture or our social structures will crumble from within. Philosophically and theologically this concept is easily refuted. If one claims that there are no absolutes, one is employing absolutes to make this claim. Again, this means the claim is self-negating. It cannot be true.

It has been spun: "Reality is that which doesn't go away when you stop thinking about it." There is a real reality. The contrary is impossible. When a person claims that there is no reality, he is a real person talking to another real person, which presupposes reality. Yet many deceived people attempt to deny the undeniable.

CHAPTER 4
WHAT'S YOUR AUTHORITY?

By What Standard?

Hear, O Israel: The LORD our God, the LORD is one! (Deuteronomy 6:4).

The starting point in a philosophical discussion on ethics is the question concerning the ground of authority. The only worldview that has an ultimate and infallible ground for the authority of ethics is Christianity. In the next few pages diverse ethical codes are listed. The first will be from Mr. Benjamin Franklin.

The Benjamin Franklin's list of Virtues:

1. *Temperance.*
2. *Silence.*
3. *Order.*
4. *Resolution.*
5. *Frugality.*
6. *Industry.*
7. *Sincerity.*
8. *Justice.*
9. *Moderation.*
10. *Cleanliness.*
11. *Tranquility.*
12. *Chastity.*
13. *Humility: Imitate Jesus and Socrates.*[33]

The question I would ask Mr. Franklin: why should anyone follow his list of virtues? His list, as well as all other non-Biblical moral codes, cannot supply the absolute reason we "ought" to follow after virtue. God commands us to hear Him and follow His word. The Hebrew word for the word "hear" is the same word that in English is "obey." God commands that we hear his commandments, and that we obey His moral law. Skeptics ridicule this idea, but the moral system that they submit in its place is relative, subjective, and self-refuting. It droops and falls under its own philosophical weight. One philosopher puts forward the notion that "morality is a system of such principals such that it is advantageous for everyone if everyone accepts and acts on it, yet acting on the system of principles requires that some persons perform disadvantageous acts."[34] Russell admitted that he distinguished between good and evil through "his own feelings."[35] Without God, and His fixed and objective moral standard, one cannot assert that the KKK, slave traders, terrorists, and mass-murderers are objectively evil. If everything that "exists is made of atoms," there can be no abstract, transcendent, and unchanging moral law. God's law establishes the foundation for the righteous civil structure, and the principled footing for the ordering of all relationships. The law cannot change with the moods of men. The moral law is not established by independent individual beliefs, fugacious feelings, convention, or Democracy.

Purpose Is Linked to Moral Law

I am absolutely convinced that the gas chambers... were ultimately prepared not in some ministry or other in Berlin, but rather at the desks and lecture halls of nihilistic scientists and philosophers (Concentration camp survivor Viktor Frankl).[36]

"And what does it amount to?" said Satan, with his evil chuckle. "Nothing at all. You gain nothing:

you always come out where you went in. For a million years the race has gone on monotonously propagating itself and monotonously re-performing this dull nonsense to what end?"[37]

O LORD, You have searched me and known me. You know my sitting down and my rising up; You understand my thought afar off. You comprehend my path and my lying down, and are acquainted with all my ways. For there is not a word on my tongue, but behold, O LORD, You know it altogether. You have hedged me behind and before, and laid Your hand upon me. Such knowledge is too wonderful for me; it is high, I cannot attain it. Where can I go from Your Spirit? Or where can I flee from Your presence? If I ascend into heaven, You are there; if I make my bed in hell, behold, You are there. If I take the wings of the morning, and dwell in the uttermost parts of the sea, even there Your hand shall lead me, and Your right hand shall hold me... for You formed my inward parts; You covered me in my mother's womb. I will praise You, for I am fearfully and wonderfully made; marvelous are Your works, and that my soul knows very well. My frame was not hidden from You, when I was made in secret, and skillfully wrought in the lowest parts of the earth. Your eyes saw my substance, being yet unformed. And in Your book they all were written, the days fashioned for me, when as yet there were none of them. How precious also are Your thoughts to me, O God! How great is the sum of them! If I should count them, they would be more in number than the sand; when I awake, I am still with You (Psalms 139:1-18).

Only the Christian worldview can supply hope. The "religion" of science cannot provide hope or purpose. Mathematics and scientific observation have demonstrated that the Second Law of Thermodynamics is a fundamental truth (all things are running down). And without God, this law of physics leaves man without a future and a hope. This law tells us that the universe is running down like a clock. One day in the distant future the whole universe will die in the whimper of an eternal heat-death. The sun, the starry hosts, and all the galaxies will be extinguished in a humming red flash. Without God, all the schemes, dreams, monuments, and attainments of mankind will be like a "cosmic sand castle" which will be toppled, subdued, despoiled, dissolved, and swept off into the sea of nothingness (unusable energy). All reality and existence will be as though it had never been and the whole universe will wear the final mark of purposelessness and oblivion, as it ebbs into the lowest vocation of quiet heat energy. The Second Law of Thermodynamics demonstrates that without God, one is left with no purpose, no meaning, and no hope.

God announces to His people that He is with them everywhere, at all times. God's will is to be our delight and purpose. The universe and our individual lives are part of the "culmination of a prefigured plan." Hopelessness is one of the dishes that the public schools serve our children. The secular schools serve up some serious atheistic-stew from the kitchen of Darwin. This is one of the reasons we have so many school shootings. Kids killing kids is a very complicated issue. Yet if students are told that they are no more than a "grown up germ," ultimately birthed by the slime of a primordial soup, they will act like slime. The schools that teach our kids that they are just "apes with Reeboks" are indirectly encouraging them to behave like the Gorilla's in the *Planet of the Apes*. This is immoral and unacceptable.

Sagacious But Illegitimate

Socrates believed that the best life is realized when the soul ponders ultimate beauty in its pure form and when it pursues knowledge of ultimate forms. This and many other theories (by Socrates as well as other philosophers) have no ultimate footing to ground their claims. They are just empty claims by individual men – though many times from very brilliant men – nevertheless, just men. Those, who believe that human existence and our universe are just "accidental afterthoughts," leave souls in despair, immersed in purposelessness. When one reads Bertrand Russell summing up life as "unyielding despair," one starts to ache for meaning and purpose. To find meaning in life, one has to look to the true and living God. He is the God of the living and He gives life purpose and meaning. Life is a sacred gift to be unwrapped everyday with the joy of a child's birthday.

The Bible tells us to do "all things for the glory of God." Holy writ notifies the world that in our life, we can have the supreme joy of knowing the Father in a loving, covenant relationship. One cannot have real meaning in this life without the Lord Jesus Christ. Emptiness, loneliness, purposelessness, and despair are the companions of those who do not seek God in Christ. A covenant life with God Almighty brings daily enrichment, enchantment, and a wonder-filled life. Doing all things for the glory of God, and enjoying Him brings a splendor-filled zest to the daily delights of nature, employment, motherhood, children, friends, God's word, prayer, and most of all in a personal relationship with Jesus our Master and Savior.

God is The God of Hope

And may the God of hope fill you with all joy and peace as you trust in Him, that you may overflow with hope through the power of the Holy Spirit (Romans 15:13).

Blessed be the God and Father of our Lord Jesus Christ, who has blessed us with every spiritual blessing in the heavenly places in Christ, just as He chose us in Him before the foundation of the world, that we should be holy and without blame before Him in love, having predestined us to adoption as sons by Jesus Christ to Himself, according to the good pleasure of His will, to the praise of the glory of His grace, by which He has made us accepted in the Beloved. In Him we have redemption through His blood, the forgiveness of sins... having made known to us the mystery of His will, according to His good pleasure which He purposed in Himself (Ephesians 1:3-9).

Hungering for the world's disjointed abstract knowledge will only lead to struggle and despair. Purpose and meaning are pursued, attained, and sustained by a hot-blooded, passionate pursuit of Jesus. The non-Christian worldview leads to Heidegger's ultimate, yet empty answer, to the problem of the meaninglessness of life, "is to stand on deck and salute" as the ocean liner sinks. He tells us to do this because it is more visually appealing than doing nothing. That's real despair. That's depressing. Thank God, it is false. Following Jesus lifts one up into a wonderful, enthralling life in the Spirit.

Neglecting or rejecting God's purpose in Christ is:

1. *Unproductive.*
2. *It leads to despair and emptiness.*
3. *It is prideful.*

The Path of Purpose and Meaning

The LORD is my shepherd; I shall not want. He makes me to lie down in green pastures; He leads me beside the still waters. He restores my soul; He leads me in the paths of righteousness for His name's sake. Yea, though I walk through the valley of the shadow of death, I will fear no evil; for You are with me; Your rod and Your staff, they comfort me. You prepare a table before me in the presence of my enemies; You anoint my head with oil; my cup runs over (Psalms 23:1-5).

Meaning, purpose, and happiness come when I:

A. *Look to God's word, follow Him and glorify Him alone (2 Timothy 3:16-17; Luke 14:27).*
B. *Decide to focus on eternal things (Colossians 3:2).*
C. *Look for things in my life that need to be changed (Psalms 119:11).*
D. *Ask others what my character flaws are (Proverbs 15:22).*
E. *Be amazed about Jesus again (Galatians 2:20)!*
F. *Trust Jesus - believe in Him for all things (John 14:1; Ephesians 3:20).*
G. *Pray (1 Thessalonians 5:17).*
H. *Look to the Gospel (Rom. 1:16; 1 Corinthians 15:3-4).*
I. *Remember happiness is not Hell (Matthew 25; Revelation 20-22).*

Nevertheless do not rejoice in this, that the spirits are subject to you, but rather rejoice because your names are written in heaven (Luke 10:20).

I have asked hundreds and hundreds of non-absolutists, from self-styled religionists to independent atheistic materialists, the following question without ever receiving a logical answer:

Mike: Is there absolute truth?

Non-Christian: No. We can't know anything for certain.
Mike: Are you certain of that?

Anything that contradicts the Biblical worldview will, at some point, be self-stultifying, self-defeating, and self-refuting. Bringing up this point is a great way to start a conversation. Do not let them change the subject. Press them on their self-refuting fallacy, and then proceed to share the law and the gospel with them. If one asserts that we can't know anything for certain, then we cannot know that for certain. If their statement is true, then it is false. If it is false, then obviously it is not true. Kant built on Socrates and Hume in promulgating the notion that one could discern and practice morality without God's revelation. Kant would have us believe we could discover ethics through the use of "pure reason." Yet a normative ethical code has not and cannot exist without God's law. There isn't a constant and universal ethical common ground among cultures or peoples. Even cultures within the same country lack ethical common ground (as we have seen in Afghanistan, Iraq, and India). Many Islamic cultures decree that it is the moral duty of faithful Muslims to blow up innocent civilians. Various pagan cultures demand the burning of widows. Some cultures demanded the sacrifice of virgins to the Aztec gods. A few Buddhist sects sanction burning oneself to death in a suicidal protest to make a political point. All these acts are evil because they contradict God's law. Only the true and living God can decree that which is good and that which is evil.

Islamic Moral Code

The Islamic moral code is an ethical system that sanctions murder and the repression of women. The main problem with Islamic morality is it has a false foundation. Allah doesn't exist. If he did exist, as a lone monad deity, love could not be part of his eternal nature. Love is the heart and motivation of true morality.

The Islamic god cannot account for love since it is not an eternal attribute of his nature. The Biblical God is love. He has loved, through all eternity, as the Father loved the Son and the Holy Spirit. Love flows to man from God's nature because love is an eternal attribute of God. Allah is a god who has commanded his followers to pursue jihad against Jews, Christians, and all other "infidels" (see Sura 8:60, 9:14, 8:12 & 17, 9:5 & 29, 2:193, 8:41, and 9:123 and Hadith 1:25, 4:196, etc.). Remember, it was Muhammad himself, who led or ordered twenty-seven warring attacks against the "infidels." He, as their supreme lawgiver, gave the order to decapitate 900 Jewish men for not receiving him as a prophet.

Some Muslims, by human standards, are descent and devout people, but they worship a false god. A god who commands them to kill non-Muslims. Jihad is a requirement for all faithful Muslims. Millions of Muslims affirm and support jihad. Jihad against Israel, America, and all non-Muslims is an important element in the worldview of large populations of Muslim people. The Koran commands: "Slay the idolaters, wherever you find them... ambush them" (Sura 9). The Arabic dictionary defines jihad: "To fight and kill in the path of Allah, the enemies of Allah, for the cause of Allah. It can also be used to mean to strive in the path of Allah."

Islam Calls Evil: Good

Orthodox Islam teaches what is unlawful, is lawful; what is ungodly, is godly; what is wicked, is virtuous; and what is unspiritual, is spiritual. Consistent and orthodox Islam is brutal and uncompromising. This is a fact. Sometimes we have to face "unhappy facts." Not liking the facts has nothing to do with their truthfulness. I may not accept something that is true because it is troubling. Yet, it is still true. If I don't like garlic, and I declare that garlic doesn't exist, the "unhappy fact" is garlic does exist. Denying the existence of garlic is wishful thinking. And asserting that Islam is a peaceful religion also is wishful thinking. My self-deception and assertion do not change that unpleasant fact. The American people have to face the grim and painful fact: pure and faithful Islam is a hateful and warring faith. Many Muslim cultures attempt to live and uphold Koranic and Hadithic injunctions. The following is an example of this reported in many major newspapers: "A tribal council in Pakistan determined that an eleven year-old boy was wrong for walking, unchaperoned, with a girl from a different tribe. His punishment for this great sin? Members of the tribal council gang-raped his 18 year-old sister... the girl was being repeatedly raped in a mud hut, hundreds of people stood outside laughing and cheering" (It was the second such judicially sanctioned rape in a week. The other girl killed herself). The reporter goes on to recall an incident that her spouse had witnessed in Islamic Pakistan: "My husband was... in Pakistan... saw a body of a young girl nearby. Her throat had been cut. They were later told that the girl had talked with a man who was not a relative."[38] Islamic "morality" is immoral and evil.

Orthodox Muslim Duty

Muslims, who suppress the wicked commandments of their god, are not being consistent with their worldview. I rejoice in the fact that some media Muslims indirectly embrace the Christian worldview by disavowing works of iniquity that the Koran commands. The great majority of Islamic scholars in the Arabian countries, as well as other Muslim nations, clearly teach their followers that it is their Muslim duty to kill those who will not receive Islam. Some Muslims may decry terrorism, just as some "Christians" may assert that Jesus did not die on the cross and rise again. One can call oneself a Christian, yet still deny the faith. I can walk into "Toys R Us" and declare that I am a toy. My declaration doesn't make it true. When a Muslim denies the call to kill non-Muslims, he denies a basic tenant of Islam. A doctrine taught and preached by the great majority of Muslims in every century since its birth. The bloodthirsty Muhammad launched and advanced Islam with the sword. Muhammad himself led numerous invasions on neighboring villages during his lifetime, while his followers engaged in fifty more. The conquered people were given the choice: conversion to Islam or death. Christians, pagans, and Jews were murdered in mass killings by the armies of Muhammad in seventh century Islam. Islam's inception is associated with war. At Islam's founding (from 623 A.D. to 777 A.D.) there were eighty-three military campaigns involving the Muslims. Over a hundred pillaging raids, wars, military ambushes, battles, and massacres spread Islam from North Africa to Spain in about a hundred years.

Islamic plundering raids continued after the seventy-seven attacks that Muhammad spearheaded or ordered. Jesus Christ ordered zero military attacks. Muhammad ordered dozens and dozens. Saint Paul commanded zero military campaigns. Muhammad organized over seventy raids. Peter, Paul, John, James, Mark, and all the Christians for the first three hundred years of Christianity, directed zero military wars. Muhammad stirred up hatred and conducted over five-dozen conquests in the name of Allah.

The Numerous Muslim Wars

The Islamic Caliphate reached from the edge of India to the borders of France. Charles Martel stopped the Muslim hordes at the battle at Tours in the eighth century. In the 630's A.D., Syria, Iraq, Egypt, and Damascus fell to the Muslim invaders that swept aside almost every remnant of Christian civilization. In the 640's A.D., Jerusalem and Persia collapsed from the hordes of Muslims hurled at their borders. Atrocities and horrific acts were leveled on many of those who did not embrace Islam. The Muslims invaded Christian lands and depopulated them by the sword and fire, plundering and pillaging the communities. The Crusades were launched to try and stop the momentum of the Islamic butchers. Many "Christians" engaged in atrocities during the Crusades in direct opposition to what Jesus taught. Mass murder of non-Muslims is commanded in Islam. Thus, the Muslims kept up their unprovoked attacks against Christian Eastern Europe and the Byzantine Empire. Islam incessantly threatened the Balkans, Austria and Hungary. The conquest of Constantinople, in 1453, saw devout Christians massacred and cut down like grass by the Muslim invaders. Holy relics were tossed into the sea or melted down. Christian diplomats, citizens, ministers, women, and children were butchered. Bodies were stacked up as high as the wall around the city. The churches were converted to Mosques, as several thousand of the massacred heads bobbed in the bay. The Muslims were motivated by jihad and dreams of a world wide Islamic conquest. Unjust war is contrary to Biblical Christianity. Unjust war is a faithful action in Islam.

> Hear, O Muslims, the meaning of life. The peak of the matter is Islam itself. The pillar is Rakatin prayer. And the topmost part is Jihad - holy war (Muhammad in the Hadith).

> Allah has promised a far richer reward for all who fight against the infidels. If they be a hundred, they shall rout a thousand of the infidels (Koran).

The Muslim Glorification of War

The glorification of war in Islam comes from their ideology that propagates the notion that the whole world is destined to become Muslim by Arab conquests. True Christianity is spread by preaching, kindness, example, morality, and active compassion for the poor. Islam expands by the sword. The date of September eleventh has historical significance that you will not hear from the liberal media or from the history books written after

1960. On September 11, 1683, the Islamic government, centered in Istanbul, tried to destroy all Christian civilization at the time of the reign of Charles III. The Muslims advanced through Eastern Europe. They almost took Vienna. The Polish King rescued it as he turned the Muslim invaders back. That was September 11, 1683. The bottomless hatred of large and diverse populations of Muslims cannot be assuaged by negotiation or compromise. The goal of throngs of Muslims is the extermination of Israel, America, and Christian civilization. Deep hatred for the West pervades most of the Islamic world, and it's fueled by Koranic injunctions. Former chief of security operations for the Strategic Air Command wrote: "One of the premises of successfully fighting a war remains: Know your enemy. The American psyche does not comprehend the concept of jihad, where merely saying *kafir* (infidel) reduces a non-Muslim man, woman, or child to something akin to a mosquito to be swatted without so much as a momentary regret."

Islamic War on Rights

The birth of Jesus Christ was the turning point in
the history of women (L. F. Servants).

The birth of Christ was the catalyst for the advancement of women's rights and the birth of Muhammad was the antithesis of those rights. Islam is not just misanthropic, it is rigorously against women's rights. The misogyny of Islam came with its birth and has not relented. When the Islamic Turks came to Vienna they were startled when they witnessed the social deference shown to women by the Christians. Islamic cruelty to women goes well beyond the culture forcing the *Chamur* on women. Islam breeds a culture that practices female genital mutilation. The young women and little girls are forced to have their clitoris removed by knives or razor blades. Many die a horrible death from this ghastly genital removal. In Egypt 6,000 girls a day have their genital organs cut away and it is a common practice in Muslim Africa, Indonesia and the Middle East (130 million women have survived this barbaric procedure).

The Palestinian homicide bombers are following the imperatives of historical Islam and most of the Islamic scholars in the Muslim world. The homicide bombers, who seek to maim, burn, and kill Jews, are following Allah and the Koran. "X-rays of suicide bombing victims often show hundreds of metallic fragments... whole nails, grotesquely embedded in the victims' bodies – literally from head to foot... Nails, screws, nuts, and ball bearings are packed by suicide bombers into their explosive vests to maximize lethal effects and to inflict unimaginable pain and suffering on innocent Jewish bodies... For the Palestinian suicide bomber, violence and the sacred are intertwined. This homicidal terrorist believes unreservedly that there can be no greater glory that inflicting measureless pain upon all Jewish bodies."[39]

The Supremacy of Christian Law over Islamic Law

Christians are murdered in many Muslim nations for practicing their religion. Black Christians in Southern Sudan have been taken as slaves by Muslims and sold in mass at the trading blocks in Mecca. Thousands of black Sudanese have been sold into slavery by Muslims. And to add to that, Islamic morality puts women into brutal slave like subjugation. Christianity liberates women. The Bible instructs us that in Christ there is "neither male nor female." Jesus went against His culture by having women as disciples. Women stayed with Jesus at the cross and He appeared first to women after His resurrection even though women were not qualified to be legal witnesses in a culture dominated by Rabbinical ideology. In Islam, marriages of old men to young girls are arranged by male relatives without the consent of the girls. In many Islamic nations, women are put into harems if they are poor; they have no rights, they have no property, and must be covered in public. Islamic scholars have fought in academia over whether or not women have souls. Islam still practices selling young girls as slaves in Northern Africa and Arabia. And Women have half as much a vote as men (Sura 4:11 and 2:282). Men are allowed to beat their wives and the Koran gives instructions on how to do this (Sura 4:34; Hadith 7.62.77). Islamic legal code, extracted from the Koran and the Hadith, instructs the citizen to drink camel urine for medical reasons, how to tie your shoes and pass teacups, how to bathe and dress. Muhammad also commands his followers to partake of a fly in one's drink as a sign of guaranteed good health. Orthodox Islam also has rules on proper bathroom hygiene that prohibits the use of toilet paper.

The supremacy of Christian law over the imbecility of Islamic law is important to our future. It's not just "two bald men fighting over a comb." The Islamic prohibitions against alcohol, pork, and the exposing of the faces of women, are all but trifles in comparison to the Koranic imperative to wage jihad against all non-Muslims.

> They have lived long and prospered. But now, we shall invade their land and curtail their borders (Koran, Sura 21:41-46).

Early Christianity grew and spread by the spoken word, peace, love, and sacrifice; it overtook the whole Roman Empire by persuasion and works of compassion. Islamic morality is the antithesis of Christian morality. Islam spread by ambush, atrocities, and forced conversions. Last century, this warring religion murdered a million and a half Armenian Christians in Turkey. You can check every century, every nation, and every era; where Islam appeared, you will find atrocities, abominations, genocide, and mass murders in the name of Allah. This is what the Koran commands. This is what the great majority of Islamic scholars have believed throughout history. This is what the majority of average Muslims believe because of the example of Muhammad, and the commandments of the Koran. It is against the law to publicly preach a non-Islamic religion in every Muslim nation. The death penalty is imposed on all who are found guilty of this "offense."

I pray that all violent religionists would affirm and embrace the Christian worldview of love, lawfulness, and peace. I would pray that they would come all the way and trust in Christ, the Prince of Peace. But today, the gloomy fact is, large populations of Muslims, in dozens of nations, want the entire world to convert to Islam, by the sword or bomb if necessary.

> Allah's messenger has commanded: fight against the unbelievers and kill them. Pursue them until even a stone would say; come here Muslim, there is an infidel hiding. Kill him. Kill him quickly (Koran, Sura 16:13).

CHAPTER 5
THE TRUE AND LIVING GOD MUST EXIST

There is No Other God Besides The Lord

"You are My witnesses," says the LORD, "And My Servant whom I have chosen, that you may know and believe Me, and understand that I am He. Before Me there was no God formed, nor shall there be after Me. I, even I, am the LORD, and besides Me there is no Savior" (Isaiah 43:10-11).

The God of the Bible is the foundation and stream for equality, love, logic, mathematics, and motion. The nature of God: the Father, and the Son, and the Holy Spirit, is the source and foundation for all these dynamics. The Islamic god is a uni-person god. Love could not have come from him because Allah didn't have anyone to love until he created the angels and mankind. Love must have an object, to be. Within the being of the true God, there has always been love. The Father loved the Son, and the Son the Holy Spirit. The Holy Spirit eternally loved both the Father and the Son. God is the precondition for love. Without the Biblical God, you cannot have eternal and infinite love. God is the precondition for equality. Within the nature and being of God, ontologically, the Father is equal to the Son, and the Son to the Holy Spirit. For one to consistently uphold and justify ontological equality between all human beings, one must base equality on a fixed, objective source; the character of the true and living God. The problem of the one and the many can only be solved by the reality of the triune God. And the problem of infinite numbers, in a finite, material world, can only be accounted for through the multi-unity of the eternal persons within the Godhead: the Father, the Son, and the Holy Spirit. God is one God in three persons, diversity in unity, unity in diversity.

> Then God said, "Let Us make man in Our image, according to Our likeness" (Genesis 1:26).

> And the LORD shall be King over all the earth. In that day it shall be: The LORD is one, and His name one (Zechariah 14:9).

Skeptics have charged Christianity with killing in the same manner that Islam has murdered. History records professing "Christians" engaging in unjust and unlawful wars. The Bible doesn't sanction unlawful acts of war. If men confess Jesus Christ, yet practice the opposite of what He taught, by definition they are not a Christian. I can tell the world I am not a drunk, but if I consistently practice drunkenness, I'm still a drunk. By God's grace, I demonstrate what I am by what I do. Jesus Christ rebuked antinomianism, upheld the law, and commanded His followers to follow Him. The consistent Christian is loving, peaceful, and a pro-nomian. It is incongruous with the Christian faith to engage in acts of terrorism. The Bible reveals that the greatest thing is love. The orthodox Muslim's duty is to kill Christians and Jews. The rightful duty of the Christian is to love all men as themselves.

Other Non-Christian Ethical Systems

> Apparently healthy, normal, pleasant young German lads, counterparts... in America would be called "fine college boys," could be and were - 1000's of them - turned quickly into cruel, course

bullies who, in uniform of the notorious S.S., flogged elderly doctors and schoolmasters into unconsciousness for the facilitating of the process of opening the jaws and purloining the gold fillings of their... victims before they were wheeled off to one of the crematory.[40]

Man – the most brutal, the most resolute creature on earth. He knows nothing but extermination of his enemies in the world (Adolph Hitler in his wicked work: *The Superiority of the Aryans*).

How do you know what is right or wrong? Many people feel the way to establish law is to study a problem and legislate what "works best." Laws that promote a moral code that "works best" are capricious. Laws that promote the greatest amount of happiness for the greatest number of people are, also, fickle and arbitrary. These laws can change. And they do not provide a standard to discern what is "happiness" or what "works best." Utilitarianism declares that law is to be based on evaluating what supplies the most utility for the most men; what provides the most happiness for the greatest number of humanity. Laws are to be legislated based on what will promote the best consequences. This notion cannot supply an ultimate and unchanging standard. It just pushes the question back one step. One must ask what is the ultimate standard that judges what is "best?"

In 2004, Las Vegas County Commissioners and members of the community gathered to debate laws that would restrict "erotic dancers." They decided to proscribe moderate rules for "lap dancing." Most of the citizens and the commissioners did not sight any moral law that would prohibit such behavior. Instead, one after another sighted pragmatic reasons to support their arguments such as: Scientific research indicates sensual touching promotes good health for the human heart. One lady who spoke was an ex-stripper, and she recounted how stripping ruined her life (research has also indicated that many serial rapists and sex offenders visit strip clubs and this eventually leads them to commit heinous sexual crimes against others). Endorsement of pragmatism raises the question: By what standard does society use to discern what works best? Through lap dancing, many men will have healthier hearts, yet, many others will be injured as an indirect or direct result of this perversion.

Pragmatic Law Leads to Evil

Laws cannot be completely based on the principle of what "works best." Pragmatism is an abstract notion and falls under its own weight. It tumbles inasmuch as the principle itself cannot be tested, studied, and found to work best. Furthermore, an absolute fixed ethical system cannot be based on what maximizes utility. The utilitarian precepts can be "Play-Doe" in the hands of righteous men or wicked men. Wicked people can decide that all manner of evil has more utility, and then pass laws based on that evil. Nazism wooed the German people in great numbers through the utilitarian application of Hitler's ideas. The majority of the German people believed that Nazism brought happiness and great industry to their country in the late 1930's and early 1940's. Yet Nazism was evil. The records of the Nuremberg Trials on Nazi war crimes states: "About a million and a half people were exterminated in Madnek... over 133,000 persons were tortured and shot... Germans... exhumed and burned corpses, and crushed their bones with machines and used them for fertilizer... Nazi conspirators mercilessly destroyed even children. They killed them with their parents, in groups, and alone... they buried the living in graves, throwing them into flames... conducting experiments on them."

Without God, nothing can supply the paradigm for universal moral absolutes. Society needs an absolute universal moral law to evaluate what is best and what is good, or it will fall into barbarism. Without God, moral choices are unclear and unintelligible. God is the only precondition for moral absolutes.

The true God is inescapable. Men may try to escape His moral decrees, but without them, life can only lead to despair and pain.

Moral Law: It's more Than a Feeling

Supreme Court justice Stephen Bryer revealed his ultimate measure for deciding law. On November 10, 2005 on *CSPAN* he conceded that he knew his ruling was right by how he "feels" in his heart. The brilliant atheist Bertrand Russell admitted that he based his ethics on how he "feels." Pol Pot felt he needed to mass-murder one million of his citizens in the killing fields; Hitler felt like murdering over 10,000 people a day and to use the skin of those murdered to make lamp shades and use their hair to make sacks. Only a moral system grounded on peremptory rational commitments to God can pronounce that mass murder is always wrong.

Ethnic Cleansing and Utilitarianism

If men are wicked with religion, what would they be without it? (Benjamin Franklin).

In claiming that the Turks were wrong in the mass genocide of one million-plus Armenians, one needs more than an ideology that establishes law based on maximum utility. The Turks thought the ethnic cleansing of the Armenians was of great benefit for most of the people in Turkey. The genocide helped the greatest number of people, as it increased and augmented the most happiness for the most people. Putting women in emotional, civil and physical bondage, makes most Muslim men, in dozens of countries, very happy. An *Associated Press* article, of March 6 2003, reported an opinion poll of the people of Russia. The poll found that 53 percent of the respondents viewed Stalin's role (he murdered some 20 to 35 million people) in Russian history as "absolutely positive" or "more positive than negative." Yet, only 33 percent said his role was "absolutely negative" or "more negative than positive." And in America, the Columbine High School murderers justified their crimes using Darwinism and wearing natural selection shirts.

What if the majority of a nation voted that killing people with big noses or large feet made them most happy? What if 51 percent voted to kill the other 49 percent who had bigger noses or larger feet? Is it wrong? By the utilitarian benchmark it is lawful and good inasmuch as it benefits the most human beings. By what standard does society measure happiness and pain? If most people are not happy and feel pain because they cannot afford steak seven days a week, does society have the moral obligation to take the people out to Sizzler every night? What if the majority of people can't afford to buy the super size meal deal at Taco Bell? Do we owe the people a big Chulupa combo with an extra-large Pepsi because this will make the most people happy? One needs an absolute moral yardstick to make law. Pragmatism and utilitarianism cannot supply this absolute standard. Philosophers fell short when they attempted to devise a obligatory criterion. The best they could come up with was the "pleasure calculus." The laborious chart did not work because it was arbitrary and could not deliver a universal and fixed moral touchstone. God has given mankind the blessing of an absolute moral law that binds all men at all times. This gift is His commandments. The absolute moral law which all censure, prohibition, civil restraint, individual rights, approbation, and righteous jurisprudence are derived. We are to reject all moral and ethical systems that are not derived from the principles of God's law.

Human Philosophy Cannot Supply
the Foundation for Ethics

The Greek ethics of pleasure is linked to a virile society, to dis-symmetry, exclusion of the other, an obsession with penetration, and a kind of threat of being dispossessed of your own energy, and so on. All that is quite disgusting.[41]

Imagine a man in the 1800's visiting a clock maker's shop every day to set his watch. He determined the time to adjust his watch from the shopkeeper's clocks. He did this to guarantee the precise time. This man was the keeper of the big town clock. But there was a problem: The clock maker adjusted his clocks every day by the time that the big town clock gave. Consequently both the clock maker and the town clock keeper had the wrong time. They lacked an exact standard. Without a precise absolute standard one cannot know what time it is, and one cannot live a moral life. A changing, imprecise human being cannot furnish the necessary absolute standard for morality. Only a perfectly precise and unchangeable God can.

You can see a lot just by observing (Yogi Berra)

Empiricism (the notion that truth is discovered by observation and the use of the five senses) also fails to supply the foundation of law because one cannot observe, hear, taste, feel, or smell a moral law. One cannot provide a fixed and certain moral ethic through empiricism. Empirical observation can be tricky. Without God's transcendent standard, why should we trust a sane man's moral observations more than a crazy person's? If we "ought" to because one is wise and one is a fool, by what standard do you judge that? And that still begs the question on why humanity "ought" to. Mental patients claim they see monsters or unicorns dancing across their sheets, yet under a materialist's empiricism the insane are on equal footing with the sagacious. Both are just organized chemicals that happen to move and speak. Thus empiricism cannot supply the reason one ought to enlist the wise over the deranged.

Rationalism (the theory that truth is found through pure

reason) cannot give an ultimate footing for moral law because reason and logic cannot provide the "ought" in ethics. Men often err in their own reasoning. And rationalists hold different views on rational standards. There is very little agreement within rationalism. Unaided human reason needs revelation from a perfect immutable God. Nihilism is also false. The notion of nihilism is unintelligible and self-defeating because it alleges that all things are meaningless. If that statement were true, then it would be meaningless, thus, it is false. Humanism has no ultimate answers. The *Humanist Manifesto II* falsely claims: "Supernatural moral commandments are especially repressive to our human need. They are immoral... " Ought we get rid of all supernatural law? If so, where does the "ought" to do good come from? Are all people everywhere bound to this humanist law? Deny the Christian worldview, and there is no accounting for an unchanging basis of "ought." The ethical model offered by the humanists cannot justify their defiance against God's moral law. They cannot account for the binding of any law. Absolute laws are independent of people's beliefs. They must exist and they must be upheld or violent crime will consume our culture as Camus wrote: "Lust when indulged becomes a killer." People may believe and affirm them, but true moral absolutes can only be justified if they come from God.

Only Christianity Can Supply A Just Moral Code

Hinduism cannot be the foundation of absolute moral law because it rejects human equality and dignity. It sanctions the burning of widows at their deceased husbands funeral pyre. It commands the faithful to care for monkeys, rats, and cows over human needs. It supplies the moral imperatives for its prejudicial caste system. The Hindu code of Manu (Sacred Law) ordains and outlines prejudice and inequality within the four main classes among the three thousand castes. The Rajput Hindu culture endorses, sanctions, and orders the marriage of children as young as two years old. Obedience means one must be married before puberty. Tribal law in some parts of Mexico allows for the rape of young girls. Sexual violence against women has a lesser penalty than stealing a cow in some Mexican towns. Usually the victim – if she goes to the authorities – gets arrested and jailed. Some modern scholars suggest that rape is morally neutral since "biological characteristics of human males are aggression and promiscuity" and this leads to rape.

Communism cannot be the foundation for universal ethics because it includes the mass murdering imperatives and actions of Stalin, Mao, and Pol Pot. The communist leaders in the twentieth century killed almost a hundred million people through communist ideology. "Joseph Stalin admitted to Winston Churchill that merely one purge had exterminated 15 million people. Stephanie Courtois' *Le Livre Noir Du Communisme* makes an impressive case for the fact that Communism's evil far exceeded even that of the Nazi's..."[42] Solzhenitsyn claimed that up to sixty million people were exterminated by Stalin and his henchmen. If there is no God, everything is permissible and nothing can be said to be wrong, depraved, or evil. Might makes right. Let the powerful take anything he wants so that the strongest may survive.

Tribal cultures cannot be the ultimate standard of law because many of those tribal people commanded cannibalism, the ambush of non-communicants, the rape and butchering of other tribes, and the mass killing of buffalo by running them off steep cliffs. The Mormon religion cannot be the bearer of moral law because their scripture sanctions polygamy, prophetic wife swapping, marriage to little girls through daughter exchanges, ambush of nonmembers, celestial incest, and racism. This is immoral because these acts break most of the Ten Commandments. The LDS Church, which claims that faithful Mormons can become gods, indirectly embraces Nietzsche when he proclaimed, "I there were gods, how could I bear it to be no god myself." That's why R.C. Sproul posits this, as he negates all the calumniators of man made law, "Christianity with its ethic... the rule of God, is or a collision course with man's dream of autonomy, self-rule. If God exists, man cannot be a law unto himself."[43] The Lord does exist and His transcendent word does supply a certain moral code. All other religious or philosophical systems lack truth and authority. It is impossible for them to be true because they cannot provide an ultimate, unchanging, and universal ground for ethics.

Many people claim that there is no absolute moral code. A university student, who has a relativistic professor (who attempts to dislodge absolute moral laws from his worldview by inculcating his class with the claim that there are no moral laws), should ask his professor if he can cheat on the next test. The professor could not prohibit him from cheating and remain consistent with his teaching that there is not an absolute moral law. Without moral laws, the student is free to cheat. And the professor cannot tell him it is wrong. The professor himself claims that there is no right or wrong, hence he cannot rebuke or penalize the cheating student based on his own worldview.

The Sermon on The Mount

Do not think that I came to destroy the Law or the Prophets. I did not come to destroy but to fulfill. For assuredly, I say to you, till heaven and earth pass away, one jot or one tittle will by no means pass from the law till all is fulfilled. Whoever therefore breaks one of the least of these commandments, and teaches men so, shall be called least in the kingdom of heaven; but whoever does and teaches them, he shall be called great in the kingdom of heaven... You have heard that it was said to those of old, "You shall not murder, and whoever murders will be in danger of the judgment." But I say to you that whoever is angry with his brother without a cause shall be in danger of the judgment. And whoever says to his brother, "Raca!" shall be in danger of the council. But whoever says, "You fool!" shall be in danger of hell fire.... Agree with your adversary quickly, while you are on the way with him, lest your adversary deliver you to the judge, the judge hand you over to the officer, and you be thrown into prison.... You have heard that it was said to those of old, "You shall not commit adultery." But I say to you that whoever looks at a woman to lust for her has already committed adultery with her in his heart... And if your right hand causes you to sin, cut it off and cast it from you; for it is more profitable for you that one of your members perish, than for your whole body to be cast into hell.... I say to you that whoever divorces his wife for any reason except sexual immorality causes her to commit adultery; and whoever marries a woman who is divorced commits adultery... You have heard that it was said, "An eye for an eye and a tooth for a tooth." But I tell you not to resist an evil person. But whoever slaps you on your right cheek, turn the other to him also. If anyone wants to sue you and take away your tunic, let him have your cloak also. And whoever compels you to go one mile, go with him two.... You have heard that it was said, "You shall love your neighbor and hate your enemy." But I say to you, love your enemies, bless those who curse you, do good to those who hate you, and pray for those who spitefully use you and persecute you... For if you love those who love you, what reward have you? Do not even the tax collectors do the same? (Matthew 5:1-46).

> If you hate your brother, the sin is like murder. It is necessary to love your enemies, not just our friends. Public prayer is its own reward. You should fast and give alms in secret.[44]

The words that Jesus spoke in the Sermon on the Mount were the highest, and most sublime ethical code ever given to the children of men. Jesus didn't "fence" the law as did Rabbinic Judaism. He asserted that all commandments of God are righteous (the least and the greatest of the commandments and must be followed. He didn't endorse the Rabbinic concept of *Katon* and *Chamur:* categories of small and great commandments. Jesus challenged us with the truth that no moral law is small; if you impute a law as small, the law will impute sin to you. Jesus taught, behind all the Mosaic laws, lie ethical and emotional realities for all men. The behind the scene mental states must be faced along with the outward obedience to the law. The enjoiners, duties, commandments, statutes, rules, and prohibitions of the Bible are to be embraced and followed inwardly and outwardly. They must be obeyed in the thoughts of the heart, and in the actions of the hands and feet.

Jesus alone is majestic and altogether lovely and perfect in holiness. And He gave us righteous law. Jesus as Lawgiver has no competition. He has no peer or equal. He has no rival, His excellencies boggle the mind. His words transcend all that has been spoken by the lips of man. Those who saw Him, fell at His feet, or raised fists to kill Him. Those who heard Him marveled and said, "Never has a man spoken like this!"

The Glow of The Golden Rule

And just as you want men to do to you, you also
do to them likewise (Luke 6:31).

The golden rule is an ethical code that infinitely surpasses the combined moral codes of all autonomous men. If it was followed completely by all: Mental health, social well being, physical safety, honor, compassion, and order would greatly increase. Prisons and police would be made obsolete. "Do unto others as you would have them do unto you." This commandment binds us to treat others with love, righteousness, goodness, and truth; just as we desire to be treated. This is what Jesus taught. No other person ever asserted this truth in a positive, proactive form. This law is a foundation for benevolence, charity, hospitals, schools, and worldwide missions.

CHAPTER 6
MORAL APPLICATION THROUGH PROPER GOVERNMENT

Personal Application of Moral Law: Self Government

To them also, as a body politic, He gave sundry judicial laws, which expired together with the State of that people; not obliging any other now, further the general equity thereof may require (Westminster Confession of Faith 19:4).

God has blessed mankind with moral reasoning power and unchanging moral principles. These principles are to be "the general rule for life." The moral law is to govern all of life. It applies to one's personal life, family and married life, church life, and civil society. All our personal and social conduct is to be regulated by the ethical truths of God's word. They reflect God's character and must be the goal of every individual. The Sermon on the Mount amplifies the application of the Ten Commandments in regard to individual conduct. Jesus, as the most moral person in history, and the one who gave the highest and best law, commands the individual to turn the other cheek, to do good to those who do you harm, to bless those who curse you and pray for those who mistreat you. All moral government must start with the individual submitting to God's moral law.

If the individual person rejects moral truth, all other moral governments are affected. The singular person is to affirm, embrace, and obey all of God's moral law. When one individual does this, goodness and righteousness trickle up to all levels of moral government. The individual's duty is the starting point in applying morality. Only Christianity can account for the need of personal morality. That is the reason, in June of 2002, Baptist leader Jerry Vines told an audience that Islam's founder was "a demon possessed child molester who had twelve wives — his last one a nine year-old girl." This personal behavior of Muhammad was immoral and evil.

A Law unto Oneself is Unlawful

Many ideologies and religions have some morals but they are inconsistent and cannot be justified within the system itself. Communists may believe it is right to lie and murder in order to promote the party. To the consistent atheist, the concept of nonmaterial law is nonsensical. The concept does not come from the material world, thus to the consistent atheist, the notion of an absolute law does not exist. Buddhist monks may believe it is good not to help the poor because suffering is just an illusion. The only consistent and righteous moral system for the individual is Christian law. It can be justified and it is impossible for it not to be true. Many Darwinians have admitted that they embraced the Theory of Evolution so they could live in sexual freedom and indulgence. These philanderers despised the sexual mores of Holy Writ because it felt like putting on a straightjacket. They rejected God's moral code so they could pursue sexual escapades and licentiousness.

Many modern Americans believe that individual moral government is autonomous (a law unto oneself). They challenge Christians with the old canard, "You shouldn't impose your morality on me!" To them a good choice or a bad choice is completely up to the individual. Of course, no one can live this way. There must be unity in all diversity. An individual cannot live just unto himself. His actions will affect others even if he lives in the wilderness alone. There are laws that bind him to refrain from setting forest fires, and prohibit him from polluting the natural habitat. The following fictional conversation is a quick way to help put away such foolish sophistry, so you can then share the love of Christ with the unbeliever:

> *Christian:* Is it wrong to commit adultery and to lie?
>
> *Autonomous Al:* You shouldn't impose your morality on me!
>
> *Christian:* Why do you want to allow the lynching of minorities, the burning down of the rain forests, the ritual-sacrifice murders of women, and the torturing of little children?
>
> *Autonomous Al:* I didn't say that!
>
> *Christian:* Yes you did. You asserted that indirectly. If you claim that no one can impose morality on other men, then no one can prohibit rape, murder, and the destroying of the environment. Your position allows arsonists, child killers, and racists to practice their own individual morality. If they believe doing those things is good, who are you, under your worldview, to forbid them to practice such crimes? It is their personal choice.

It is easy to dislodge the false notion that one cannot impose morality on others. All our civil law asserts what is right and what is wrong through its prohibitions and its statutes. Real freedom comes to the one who submits to God's moral law. Under just law and its righteous application, citizens are safe, productive, and civil. Morality must be imposed on mankind. Even those who deny this truth, must set up laws to advance and protect their unlawful worldview. It is impossible for an individual or a culture to live without the imposition of moral law.

Family Government

> Values are personal... your value system may be
> very similar, or it may be different from ours. The
> important thing, we feel, is that parents
> consciously develop their own set... of values.[45]

> When morality is reduced to personal preference
> and when no one can be held morally
> accountable, society quickly falls into disorder.
> Entertainers churn out garbage...; politicians tickle
> our ears while picking our pockets; criminals
> terrorize our city streets; parents neglect their
> children... We must ask people to face the stark
> choice: either a worldview that maintains that we
> are inherently good or a worldview that
> acknowledges a transcendent standard and our
> accountability before a holy God.[46]

Family government is built upon individual government. It is
the second aspect of the structure of government and culture.
Relationship and marriage ethics may be the most controversial in
our postmodern culture. Much of our culture affirms that
"anything goes" when it comes to family and relationships. The
moral law and its application are labeled by many as medieval
and draconian. The Bible commands the wife to submit to her
own husband and the husband to love his wife as Christ loves the
church. This is very unpleasant to feminists and to many in
society who believe in a non-Christian worldview. Most people,
who reject the Biblical call to submission, do not have a real
understanding of God ordered submission. Images of the Taliban
and wife beaters come to the mind of a lot of men and women in
our nation when the subject of submission is discussed.

A Conversation on Submission

One night at a restaurant (a response to a Christian brother who confessed that he forgot to instruct a potential girlfriend on the role of a godly wife), I had the opportunity to ask a young waitress what she thought about the notion of the submission of a wife to her own husband:

> *Mike:* Can I ask you a question about relationships between men and women?
>
> *Waitress:* Uh, I , Uh, yes.
>
> *Mike:* Do you think a Christian man should mention the doctrine of the wife submitting to her husband before they start their relationship?
>
> *Waitress:* Uh, what do you mean? (she was caught off guard by the question, I'm sure she never had a customer ask her that question before).
>
> *Mike:* Well, my friend here is a strong Christian, and he is looking for a Christian wife. He knows a gal who just got saved, and she probably doesn't know much about her responsibilities as a Christian wife. I mentioned to him that he should teach her about the duty and delight that the wife has in submitting to her husband. As a young single lady, do you think it would be too forward for him to discuss this subject with her?
>
> *Waitress:* Well. I don't believe that women should be forced to do things against their will and be controlled by their husband. I do not think a man has the right to treat his wife like a slave or abuse his wife for any reason.
>
> *Mike:* The Bible doesn't teach that submission is a form of slavery or abuse. The word of God instructs the wife to submit to her husband in all things, but the husband has the duty and joy to

love his wife as Jesus loved the church. He must be willing to lay down his life for his spouse, just as Jesus Christ died for us on the cross because of His great love for His elect. True submission is part of the wonderful role that the wife is privileged to embrace. In making a decision, the man and wife are to discuss and pray about major decisions. When there is a disagreement, the husband is to listen to his wife, pray about the decision, when possible, lawful, and prudent, even serve her in many of her wishes. Yet if after much thought, reflection, and prayer, they still disagree; the husband has the final word and makes the decision. The wife is to joyfully submit as she trusts God's holy word in the decision. Remember, the husband has the most difficult task. He is, without excuse, to love his wife with a God-kind of love as he follows Jesus and leads his family.

Waitress: Well, I think I understand and I do not totally disagree, but...

Mike: Well the bottom line is we are to follow God's word. And many times we all have failed and sinned. Jesus Christ came down from heaven to die on the cross and rise again on the third day. All those, who repent and turn to Him in faith, go to heaven by grace alone. Trust in him. We really appreciate your time.

The confused look on the waitress' face told quite a tale. The tale that many families affirm. That is a story of autonomy (self-rule or self-law). All humans have the propensity to want to do things their own way. Many feel this is freedom. But following God, in all our loving relationships, results in true freedom. Judge Samuel Leibowitz, in his interview with David Frost in 1970, lamented about the past generation when "there was a father image, and the child was taught to respect authority. The authority of the parent, the authority of the policemen, and the authority of the teacher... there was respect. There was order."[47] If one rejects the moral code that is to guide the family, this rebellion will also affect civil society. Individual government, family government, church government, and civil government are all interconnected. Weakness in one sphere will result in weakness in the other spheres. Immoral individuals will lead to immoral families, which will lead to immoral churches, which will lead to an immoral civil society. A moral culture must start with the individual and the family.

Church Government

> We don't expect children to discover the principles of Calculus on their own, but some would give them no guidance when it comes to ethics, morality and values (Ronald Reagan).

> The law of God is entire. *Lex Est Copulative* [the law is connected]. The first and second tables are knit together; piety to God, and equity to our neighbor. Those two tablets which are joined together must not be put asunder... God wrote both tables, and our obedience must set a seal to both.[48]

Churches are to teach their members the law of God. They are to instruct their members in the ways of the Lord and exhort them to teach their family God's moral code. Preachers are to make the clear distinction between justification and sanctification. All Christians must understand that keeping God's law doesn't save their soul, but faith in Christ alone saves them. And the Christian is to follow God's law out of gratitude and love.

If you love Me, you will keep My commandments (John 14:15).

This love cannot exist until we have tasted the goodness of God. For as long as we conceive of God as being opposed to us, of necessity we will flee from Him... we must realize that he is our Father and Savior, that he only wants to be favorable to us. Thus once we have tasted his mutual love which he reserves for us, then we will be motivated to love him as our Father. For if this love is in us, then there will be no doubt that we will obey him and that this law will rule in our thoughts, affections, and in our members.[49]

The Christian is to be taught that obedience is to be motivated by love. The believer is to follow God's law because he loves God and his fellow man. God is good and loving. This truth infuses obedient love into the believer's heart, by the power and person of the Holy Spirit, through faith. If you love Jesus, you are called to follow His moral law. If a church loves Jesus, it is going to instruct and admonish its members to follow God's law. Mankind is obliged to honor the following authorities:

1. God Almighty

And God spoke all these words, saying, I am the LORD thy God, which have brought thee out of the land of Egypt, out of the house of bondage. Thou shall have no other gods before me. Thou shall not make unto thee any graven image, or any likeness of any thing that is in heaven above, or that is in the earth beneath, or that is in the water under the earth: Thou shall not bow down thyself to them, nor serve them: for I the LORD thy God am a jealous God, visiting the iniquity of the fathers upon the children unto the third and fourth generation of them that hate me; and showing mercy unto thousands of them that love me, and keep my commandments. Thou shall not take the name of the LORD thy God in vain; for the LORD will not hold him guiltless that takes his name in vain (Exodus 20:1-7).

2. Scripture

All scripture is given by inspiration of God, and is profitable for doctrine, for reproof, for correction, for instruction in righteousness: That the man of God may be perfect, thoroughly furnished unto all good works (2 Timothy 3:16-17).

3. The Church

If your brother sins against you, go and show him his fault, just between the two of you. If he listens to you, you have won your brother over. But if he will not listen, take one or two others along, so that every matter may be established by the testimony of two or three witnesses. If he refuses to listen to them, tell it to the church; and if he refuses to listen even to the church, treat him as you would a pagan or a tax collector. I tell you the truth, whatever you bind on earth will be bound in heaven, and whatever you loose on earth will be loosed in heaven. Again, I tell you that if two of you on earth agree about anything you ask for, it will be done for you by my Father in heaven. For where two or three come together in my name, there am I with them (Matthew 18:18-20).

And the multitude of them that believed were of one heart and of one soul: neither said any of them that ought of the things which he possessed was his own; but they had all things common. And with great power gave the apostles witness of the resurrection of the Lord Jesus: and great grace was upon them all. Neither was there any among them that lacked: for as many as were possessors of lands or houses sold them, and brought the prices of the things that were sold, and laid them down at the apostles' feet: and distribution was made unto every man according as he had need (Acts 2:32-35).

Whiles it remained, was it not thine own? And after it was sold, was it not in thine own power? Why has thou conceived this thing in thine heart? Thou has not lied unto men, but unto God (Acts 5:40).

 A. Elders: See: 1 Peter 5:1, 5:5; 1 Timothy 3:1-7, 5:17.
 B. Deacons: See: 1 Timothy 3:8-13; Acts 6.

Civil Government

I do not know precisely how people can start feeling for their neighbors again... But I do have a good place to start. It's something we all know by heart, yet rarely give it the attention it deserves. It is the golden rule.[50]

The Free Fruition of such liberties, immunities,

and privileges of humanity, civility, and Christianity call for as due to every man... without impeachment and infringement, has ever been and ever will be the tranquility and stability of churches and commonwealths (The Puritan's First Code of Massachusetts, 1641).

The signers of the Declaration of Independence... went on to remind the world that the people were "endowed by their Creator with certain unalienable Rights." In closing they wrote, "And for the support of this declaration, with firm Reliance on the Protection of Divine Providence, we mutually pledge to each other... Thus, despite their varied faiths... our founders joined together in invoking the aid of one Creator and share values they derived from their belief in God."[51]

Max Dimont wrote that the law of Moses "was the first truly judicial, written code, and eclipsed previous known laws with its passion for justice, its love for democracy... These laws of Moses are designed to safeguard national unity... individual rights... The lofty framework of these laws permitted the emergence of the democratic form of government."[52]

In God I have put my trust; I will not fear. What can flesh do to me?... In God I have put my trust; I will not be afraid. What can man do to me? (Psalms 56:4-11).

Civil government should be based on the general equity of the law of God. It should flow from the lawful obedience of the individual, the family unit, and the church. The Founding Fathers formed the three main branches of the federal government to create a means to restrain evil human impulses, and guard justice through its checks and balances. They built the government this way because of the scriptural truth of the depravity of man. All men are sinners and have the propensity to do wicked acts if left unchecked and unrestrained. One cannot trust the executive branch, unless it is checked by the legislative and judicial branches, and accountable to the people. The Biblical doctrine of the depravity of man was the foundation for the checks and balances that the Founding Fathers put into the American government.

In the past, the general equity of the moral code exegeted from the Bible was the goal of Christians and Jews. The Mishnah (Second Temple Jewish legal code) was the inconsistent attempt of Rabbinic Judaism to codify law by the *Tannaim* (teachers). It was arranged by Rabbi Judah the Prince. And Hillel, Shammai, and Gamaliel were some of those who opined in the pages of the Mishnah and the Talmud. The Jewish courts of the *Beth Din* applied jurisprudence to the Jewish people from the time of Moses until the destruction of the Temple in 70 A.D. They also had a Supreme court in the Sanhedrin, which legislated and adjudicated national law and there were local Jewish courts that gave decisions of *Halachah* (points of law). The Mishnah, drawing the principles from the Bible, instituted local courts and circuit courts. Similar courts were later adopted by the Christian Church. These scriptural precepts were instituted into civil law by the early American Puritans and the Founding Fathers of America. In theory, God's word is the moral pattern for Rabbinical thought and for U.S. legal theory.

One Nation Under God

When the providential hand of our heavenly Father delivered and birthed America, our forefathers engraved a slogan on the soul and currency of this great nation. They inscribed the words of King David "In God We Trust." Today when our government hires psychics and locks up Christians; when it throws out Bibles and brings in metal detectors in our schools; when it systematically kills innocent babies and elects serial fornicators; our currency still declares: "In God we Trust." Our actions often contradict our motto, but it is still our nation's creed.

Many of us know a time when there was an America where children could walk to the park without fear of molestation and abduction. Where pot was limited to something you cooked in. Where grass was mowed without bong or smoke, and coke was only a soft-drink. Where closets were for clothes and prayers and not for people to come out of. That nation is not completely fossilized, but it has enough dead material infused in it to warrant life saving surgery. Every $20 bill has "In God We Trust" printed over the picture of the White House.

The profession: "In God We Trust" means that the man in the White House or in the farm house and in the police station should trust in God and not man. God will not be mocked. A man will reap what he sows. It seems that America has put off the flag, mom, and apple pie and replaced them with gays, movies, and Playboy. Our country must repent and turn fully to God. Twice in Psalms 56, King David confirms and submits his trust in Almighty God. Our forefathers lived, fought, and died for this simple transcendent slogan: "In God We Trust." They fought and died so you and I could have civil liberties: freedom of speech and religion and the freedom to praise Christ, the freedom to preach Christ and the freedom to follow Christ; privately and publicly.

George Washington warned his countrymen that it was impossible to rightly govern without God and the Bible. Abraham Lincoln considered the Bible to be the best gift God has given man. Today, Washington and Lincoln would be told to muzzle it because God and the Bible are politically incorrect in our everything goes ultra-tolerant, free for all society. Our prayer and our focus must be to see our city, state, and country embrace the Bible. As Patrick Henry remarked, "The Bible is worth more tha all the other books that have ever been printed." We cannot say, "In God We Trust" and live in open rebellion against the law of God. The Bible is God's word. It is God's standard for pleasing the Lord. If we want to stay the Lord's hand of judgment, we must choose life. We must lift up the gospel and let freedom reign. If we want the blessings of God, it is essential that we go back to our roots.

The wicked shall be turned into hell, and all the nations that forget God (Psalms 9:17). The Bible says that all nations that forget the Lord God are turned toward hell. Some trends in this country are anti-God, anti-Christ, and anti-scripture. Bible believers are made out to be dangerous people by the godless. They are called extremists, radicals, ultra-right wing, and fundamentalists. But the season is here for the righteous to notify the world: enough is enough! Jesus Christ is the King, eternal and immortal, the only wise God. From the rising of the sun to the setting of the sun; from the streets to the beach; from our homes to our parks: Jesus Christ is Lord of all and He is our boss.

> Submit yourselves to every ordinance of man for the Lord's sake, whether to the king as supreme (1 Peter 2:13).

The Solution: Prayer, Preaching, and God's Power

Prayer has never been an option, it is a joyful duty. Prayer is a must for this nation. My prayer is that God will remove the wicked from office.

> Let every soul be subject to the governing authorities. For there is no authority except from God, and the authorities that exist are appointed by God. (Rom 13:1).

Recall the story of Nebuchadnezzer. He had a dream, but he

forgot it, so he commanded his impotent sorcerers and astrologers to ascertain what was the content of his dream: They could not do it. Daniel prayed and prayed, and God revealed the king's dream and interpretation to Daniel. Notice the manner in which Daniel praises God: "Daniel answered and said: 'Blessed be the name of God forever and ever, for wisdom and might are His'" (Daniel 2:20).

> Who removes kings? God.
> Who raises kings? God.

Scripture teaches that God Almighty controls the president's heart like water.

> Who controls every senator's heart? God.
> Who controls ever mayor's heart? God.
> Who controls every judge's heart? God.
> God is in control.

The doctrine of God's Providence was of utmost importance in the birthing of the United States of America. All historical events are under God's providential hand as He acts through human agencies. Laws alone will not change our society. Society will change when hearts change first. Only Jesus Christ and His gospel can change people.

On July 4th 1776, The Declaration of Independence proclaimed: "We hold these truths... that all men are created equal, that they are endowed by their Creator with certain unalienable rights... Appealing to the supreme judge of the world... and for the support of this declaration, with reliance or the protection of divine providence."

Jesus came to Galilee, preaching the gospel of the kingdom of God, and saying, "The time is fulfilled, and the kingdom of God is at hand. Repent, and believe in the gospel" (Mark 1:14-15) Thus, the largest institution on the planet is the church. The kingdom that contains the most citizens is the church. The association with most men is the church of Jesus Christ. Not any one denomination, but the collective body that professes Jesus Christ as Lord and Savior in America. A 2003 *Gallup Poll* found the percentage of people confessing to be Born-again Christians is 46 percent. That is way up from 33 percent from the early 1990's. That is about 135 million people proclaiming salvation in Jesus Christ as Savior.

Education has Increased:
Universal All-Gender Education Results from Christianity

Christianity is and has been the main vehicle in education. The Lord commands believers: Go and make disciples (students) of all nations. The first Christian adults were prepared for baptism as catechumens: those catechized (discipled) with doctrine. Catechism schools were established by Justin Martyr in Ephesus and Rome in 150 A.D. Girls as well as boys went to school. This was almost unheard of in Pagan civilization. Christianity's aim was universal education. Cathedral and episcopal schools flourished in the fourth to eighth century. They were maintained by pastors and taught the Trivium: Grammar, Rhetoric and Logic. Without education (making disciples) there is no Christianity. Without Christianity, there is no universal education. Because universal education is a moral aim, education presupposes morality because morality presupposes Christianity. Education for both genders is a moral notion. Again, the precondition for morality is God and His word. Jesus taught women, the Apostles taught women, as did the church. Universal education could not come from pagan nations like Greece and Rome because they taught class elitism and rejected equal rights between men and women.

Martin Luther aimed for an educational system that was free and unrestricted for both genders and all social classes, without distinction. Today, worldwide education is at an all time high. More people write, work on computers, and study than ever before. Because of Christianity and its influence, universal education is increasing every decade as an outgrowth of Biblical practice.

Christianity started the first schools for the blind.

Christianity started the first schools for the deaf.

Christianity started the first schools for the handicapped.

In ancient Greece, blind babies were tossed into the sea. If they were hidden and found later, they would be made galley slaves and the girls forced into prostitution. Louis Braille, a devout Christian in the 16th century, invented his Braille system for the blind so the blind could read. The Greeks had their philosophers groping for truth, truth they said did not really exist. But they had no permanent university. St. Benedict of Nursia opened the first university in 528 A.D. University of Bologna opened it's doors in 1158 A.D. as the first modern university and Paris in 1270 A.D. and on and on. This carried over to the US inasmuch as all the early colleges and universities in America were founded by Christians. In 1934: 92 percent of the 182 colleges and universities were founded by Christian denominations.

Modern Medicine Started through Christianity

Medical advances started and flourished because of Christianity. No other worldview could supply the conditions for the medical research. Islam forbids autopsies and investigating dead bodies, thus their medical science was stalled. Hindu's taught that disease and physical affliction should not be interfered with by medical intervention because the afflicted need their disease and pain to relieve Karma. Only Christians followed a

98

healing Savior and worshiped a God who heals and declares that life is sacred and should be protected and the sick cared for:

> I was naked and you clothed Me; I was sick and you visited Me; I was in prison and you came to Me. Then He will answer them, saying, Assuredly, I say to you, in as much as you did not do it to one of the least of these, you did not do it to Me (Jesus).

Ancient historian Dionnysius tells us that "Pagans thrust aside anyone who was sick and treated them with utter contempt until they died." Only the Christians nurtured and nursed the crippled and deformed. The pagans drowned children who were weakly and abnormal. The nursing profession was started in the second century by Bennignus of Dijon in 325 at the council of Nicea. The bishops were directed to establish a hospice in every city that had a cathedral. They nursed, healed, and cared for them. Christians built the first major hospital in 369 A.D. in Cappadocia. By 750 A.D. the spread of Christian hospitals covered the whole Christian world. By the 1500's there were 37,000 monasteries that nursed the sick. Cortez founded the first hospital in America in 1524: "The Jesus of Nazareth Hospital" to care for the sick. Hospitals were built for the colonists and the native Indians. Most hospitals even today have a Christian name on them (Baptist Hospital, Presbyterian Hospital, St. Luke's Hospital, etc.). Mental hospitals were founded by Christians in 321 A.D. and the Red Cross was started by a devout Christian.

Justification for a Just Civil Law

Without God, there is no justification for a just civil law. God is the precondition for all forms of government, including civil government. The Westminster Confession of Faith teaches that everything that mankind needs for life and justice is "either expressly set down in Scripture, or by the good and necessary consequence may be derived from Scripture." Without God's word, society can call good, bad and bad, good. The leaders can decree that evil is righteousness, and righteousness is evil. Some nations have legalized child pornography and prostitution. And these perverted behaviors have become financially rewarding "tourist industries." One cannot call pornography or prostitution evil, if you are basing your judgment of good and evil on what works best or helps the most people. Nations need a standard that transcends humanity and provides the moral foundation that gives justice "for all."

Nature's Law or God's Nature

Many within academia claim that ethics should come by means of Natural Law. Yes, God has written His law on the hearts of all men. But can we subscribe to the laws of nature? Should we imitate a queen-bee who destroys her daughters when they are hatched? Should we follow the ways of the male grizzly's morality who attacks the young cub of another bear and tries to eat the little live Teddy-bear? Should we form laws based on the black widow who eats her mate? Society cannot form a just moral code from the tooth and claw of nature. Nature's main thrust is survival of the fittest. If this natural dynamic is to be the main element of our culture's morality then we should kill all the weak, take advantage of the women, and murder all our competition. This would be evil because God's law reveals it is and we are to live and make laws based on the nature of God and not raw nature. God's nature is good, righteous, holy, and compassionate. Raw wild nature is kill or be killed. Thus good law is based on the nature of a good God.

An Eye for an Eye

Modernity often tags the law that required a tooth for a tooth and eye for an eye as almost Islamic style and draconian. They suggest that these laws are cruel and unusual. That is the exact opposite of the true effect. These laws were given by God as an act of mercy based on fairness and equity. In ancient cultures, kings and authorities would often impose extreme and harsh penalties for minor crimes. Today Islamic law chops off hands of thieves. This is not an eye for an eye. A hand is worth a lot more than a loaf of bread. Thus God stepped in and decreed that fair and just penalties must be imposed on crimes. A tooth for a tooth. Not a death sentence or the loss of your wife because you took an apple. An eye for an eye, not your home or your four camels for drunkenness. Much of our past laws were based on this principal.

In Tyler, Texas a jury sentenced a man to 16 years in prison for shoplifting a one dollar candy bar. Law and order must be established, but sentencing must be based on justice. The Smith County assistant district attorney Jodi Brown defended the verdict by reminding people that it was "a king-size" Snickers that was stolen. This is an unusual case because most sentencing problems are too lenient in America. Light punishment, probation for rape or five years in prison for murder, are the dominant errors we see in modern sentencing.

Christians should make the distinction between civil law and forgiveness found in Christ. A convicted criminal is to serve his sentence even if he becomes a Christian. The sincere incarcerated criminal is forgiven and pardoned by God through faith in the gospel, but he still must do his time. King Louis XV pardoned his cousin Comte de Charolais after Charolais shot a man on a roof for the sheer pleasure of watching him fall to the ground and die. In the pardon decree, the king added the always looming condition: "Let it be understood that I will similarly pardon anyone who shoots you." A fair and just sentence is essential for a civil government. If the courts are too indulgent and weak or if they are inclined to apply strict and iron handed punishments, justice will not be served.

Evangelism

Morality is a great tool for witnessing. You can start witnessing to an unbeliever with the following question: Are there objective, universal, unchanging moral laws? If they say "no," you then demonstrate the impossibility of that notion. If they answer in the affirmative and assert that there are absolute moral codes, you then ask them what is their standard? At that point, you demonstrate that the Bible is the only possible standard for moral law. Next you should instruct them about the reality of heaven. Teach them that heaven is perfect, God is perfect, and no one can live with God in heaven if they have sin on their record. Thus you first press the harshness of the law on them. They need to see the doom that is awaiting them without the gospel.

The Best Pitch

Satchel Paige told the Hall of Fame pitcher Nolan Ryan that his best pitch was the "bow tie." Ryan asked him, "What was that?" Paige told him it was a fast ball right by the batter's neck. That pitch would put the batter in fear and on his back heels. And this would allow the pitcher to strikeout the shaky batter with a curve-ball. Our "bow tie" fastball and best pitch is the holy law of God. It will stop up the mouths of the unbeliever, put fear in his heart, and put him off balance for the gospel curve-ball. The law is the tool God gave us to demonstrate the unbeliever's need of the gospel. As the Lutheran catechism asks: "Am I a sinner? Answer: Yes. How do I know that I am a sinner? Answer: By the Ten commandments." These are simple and powerful answers fo the lost. The following was a conversation that I had at a taco shop with an International Boston Church of Christ cult member:

I.B.C.O.C. Member: Hi, what are you reading?

Mike: It's a book about God.

I.B.C.O.C.: Really, I'm studying about God also.

Mike: Are you a Christian?

I.B.C.O.C.: Yes.

Mike: Can I ask you how a person makes it to heaven when they die?

I.B.C.O.C.: Well, you get baptized and you obey God's word.

Mike: Are you a member of the International Boston Church of Christ?

I.B.C.O.C.: Yes, how did you know that?

Mike: I have talked to a lot of folks who belong to that movement. Can I ask you a difficult question?

I.B.C.O.C.: Yes.

Mike: I don't want to hurt your feelings, but did you know that your church is considered a cult by all the counter-cult organizations?

I.B.C.O.C.: Yes, but what is a cult?

Mike: Your group teaches that only completely obedient members of your organization, who are baptized by your ministers, can go to heaven. This is really sad. It is similar to what other cults teach like the Mormons and the Jehovah's Witnesses. Look up the word cult on the Internet, and just about every organization that ministers to cults asserts that your group is, in fact, a cult. Let me ask you another question: Have you heard of the Biblical term justification?

I.B.C.O.C.: No.

Mike: That is really bad. The Bible declares the doctrine of justification by grace alone from Genesis through the Psalms, Romans, and to the book of Revelation. It is one of the most important truths a Christian must know and believe. Justification is a legal term that means the believer

MICHAEL A ROBINSON

in Christ is declared righteous based on who Jesus is, and what He did on the cross by grace alone, through faith alone. If you believe you can make it to heaven by your baptism, and works, you are deceived and lost.

I.B.C.O.C.: So all you have to do is believe and you can live in sin?

Mike: No. The Bible teaches that one is saved by grace alone, through faith alone, because of Christ alone. Yes, one is saved through faith alone, but not a faith that remains alone. When Jesus saves someone, a real Christian loves Jesus and wants to follow Him. The Christian follows the Lord and obeys His law. He doesn't do this to find a way to make it to heaven by his works, but because he loves Jesus. We obey God out of gratitude forasmuch as He saved us. Obedience is a fruit of justification, but our works in no way get us to heaven. Have you kept the Ten Commandments perfectly?

I.B.C.O.C.: No, nobody does.

Mike: Have you kept the Sermon on the Mount perfectly? In this, Jesus commands you to turn the other cheek, to go the extra mile, to pray for those who persecute you, to do good to those who mistreat you, and to not look upon someone with lust.

I.B.C.O.C.: Of course not, everyone has sinned.

Mike: In Matthew 5:48, Jesus commands us to be perfect. In fact He commands us to "be perfect as your Heavenly Father is perfect." This commandment is unyielding. Absolute perfection is the only way one can get to heaven. Heaven is perfect and God is perfect. And no one with sin can live there for eternity. To make it to the perfect heaven, God requires you and I to follow these commandments perfectly, all the time. Yet you admit that you haven't kept them perfectly. That should make you shudder and tremble with fear. So what's your answer for someone to make it to a perfect heaven, when no one has perfectly kept the Ten Commandments or the Sermon on the Mount?

I.B.C.O.C.: Uh, I don't know.

Mike: The answer is what I already mentioned. That you must turn from your ways and cast yourself totally upon the mercy of God in Christ. Turn in faith to Jesus. Trust His work on the cross and His resurrection to fully save you. When we trust Christ, we are justified. We are declared righteous and perfect in relation to God's law. God rinses our sins away and imputes to the believer the perfect righteousness of Christ. This allows the believer to enter a perfect, righteous heaven when he dies. No other religion offers this grace. No other religion has an answer to the sin problem. Heaven is perfect and we are not. How do we get in? Only through God's grace through trusting in Christ alone. You see, your religion is just like all the other 30,000-plus religions of the world. They all, all of them, teach what your group does. To get to heaven, paradise, nirvana, or escape the karmaic cycle, one must do good works. All of them teach this, as does your church. Only true Christianity declares that you can be saved by grace alone. You know, I have told you some very difficult things, some very unpleasant things. I do not want to hurt your feelings, and I do not want you to dislike me, but I would do anything possible to keep you from going back to that group. I beg you and plead with you to leave that group.

I.B.C.O.C.: Well, I have to go.
Mike: I hope we see each other here again. Here is a card to the church I attend. I hope to see you again in the future.

The Absolute Certain Argument

The consequence of affirming that God doesn't exist is to assert that the world is unintelligible and unknowable. That proposition is impossible because it is self-refuting. If the world is unintelligible and unknowable, then that statement also would be unintelligible, unknowable, and inconsistent, hence, it would be false. This consequence leads to the truth that God is the ground and foundation of knowledge. Unless Christianity is true, we can know nothing of reality. If we can know nothing of reality, we cannot know that proposition. Unless the God of revelation is and has spoken, human knowledge has no intelligible basis.

Harry Blaimires commented, "The Old and New Testament... No one can pretend it isn't there. Everyone who is concerned with the meaning of life, and the destiny of the human race will have to take it into account." God's word declares that life must revolve around Him. We must have no other gods before Him. All men have a destiny that will find its consummation at the judgment seat of Christ. Self-deceivers can pretend that God doesn't exist. but God lives. Those, who pretend He hasn't spoken, live a life that is contradictory and confusing. Their life will end one day and they will give an account for their life. This truth must consistently remain in front of our eyes. We should live and move before the face of God. This is our duty and our joy.

There are many professional skeptics and scoffers in our culture who marshal their full-bore foulness to defend atheism. The men who stroke their tobacco stained beards and try to act clever so they can employ their acerbic wit to attack God and His Christ. They are truth "falsifiers." They become experts at wishful thinking and self-deception. They have elaborate tools and arguments that instruct the blind how to stay in the dark, while professing to make them wise.

Atheism Depends on Theism

One skeptic argued "belief in the incarnation is clearly unjustified. Not only is the evidence for the incarnation lacking, but it is incoherent and conceptually problematic." That statement lacks evidence and is more than problematic. The anti-theistic cannot even account for the reality of evidence or the discovery of apparent problems. He must stand on the Christian worldview to discuss evidence and problems. Only Christianity can have a justified basis for the evaluation of evidence and the intelligent identification of problems. The skeptic's "case" is unintelligible because his assertion disqualifies itself. Thus his atheism is self-defeating like all systems that reject God's word. Atheism proclaims physicalism, that all reality is composed only of physical material. Yet that proclamation is not made up of anything physical or material. The atheist's view cannot support or justify itself. Atheism is a nonphysical system that teaches that the nonphysical does not exist. Yet the anti-theist's critiques of theism are not physical in and of themselves. It pops its own philosophical balloon. Proposing any philosophy, including that only the physical world exists, is a nonphysical exercise. When one propagates anything, one is affirming that God lives through his use of nonphysical assertions and critiques. To claim to be a physicalist, one is actually assenting to anti-physicalism.

Proof is Built on Absolute Truth

One important area of "proof" is the messianic prophecies that were fulfilled by Jesus Christ. The Tenach (Old Testament) foretold the coming of the Messiah in exact detail. The text was written centuries before the coming of Jesus, and it predicted over

300 prophecies about Him. No other founder of any religion can provide a similar broadly circulated prophetic record of his life written down centuries before his birth. Joseph Smith, Ellen G. White, Krishna, Muhammad, and the Dali Lama cannot supply a widely transmitted, preexisting written record that accurately predicted the details of their life.

The three hundred-plus prophecies of the coming Messiah were the predicted and predestined acts of God. The Lord forecasted events and historical facts about the coming of Jesus prior to His birth. All these predictions came true in the birth, life, death, and resurrection of Jesus of Nazareth. No other leader or prophet had predictive material written about their life recorded before they were born. Jesus had over three hundred predictions about His life that were fulfilled in exact detail. His virgin birth was predicted about seven hundred years before He was born in Isaiah 7:14: "So, the Lord Himself shall give you a sign. Behold, the virgin will conceive and shall bring forth a son, and they shall call His name Emmanuel." His place of birth was forecasted in Micah 5:2: "And you, Bethlehem... out of you He shall come forth to Me, to become Ruler in Israel, He whose goings forth have been... from eternity." God prophesied the Palm Sunday entrance recorded in Zechariah 9:9: "Rejoice greatly, O daughter of Zion! Shout, O daughter of Jerusalem! Behold, your King is coming to you; He is just and having salvation, lowly and riding on a donkey, a colt, the foal of a donkey."

The Cross Foretold

Christ's death on the cross was foretold before that form of execution was even invented by Persia. Psalms 22:1-16 announces the crucifixion hundreds of years before it happened: "My God, my God, why have You forsaken me... But I am a worm, and no man a reproach of men, and despised by the people. All who see me laugh me to scorn; they shoot out the lip; they shake the head saying, He trusted on the LORD; let Him deliver him; let Him rescue him, since He delights in him! I am poured out like water, and all my bones are spread apart; my heart is like wax; it is melted in the midst of my bowels and You have brought me into the dust of death. For dogs have circled around me; the band of spoilers have hemmed me in, they have *pierced my hands and my feet"* (italics added). This evidence is overwhelming. But the truth is even more certain and compelling than compiling great blocks of evidence to prove the truth of Christianity. The argument for Jesus Christ is certain. Without God, one cannot provide the necessary preconditions for truth and certainty.

God's Existence is Certain

Without God, one cannot account for anything. God is the precondition for logic, morality, mathematics, and everything else in the cosmos. This is the certain argument that is absolutely true. The truth is simple, and it is powerful. You must understand that the unbeliever needs to hear it echo and reecho. When you are talking with a skeptic be unremitting with this apologetic.

The great thing about employing the "argument from the impossibility of the contrary" is that it grows in power when the unbeliever attacks it. The argument grows in force because the unbeliever must use logic to make his intellectual challenge. Logic requires God. Only Christianity supplies the necessary *a priori* conditions for logic. Thus every time an unbeliever rationally attacks God he is demonstrating that God lives. Without God, he cannot make any rational assertion. So every time he says anything, he is increasing the clear force of the argument that declares God lives. The unbeliever will attempt to fire intellectual weapons at the "argument from the impossibility of the contrary." Yet all their attacks will only be consumed by the truth, as the defense of the truth grows stronger and larger. There is nothing a skeptic can assert without ultimately relying on theism since God alone provides the preconditions for the laws of logic. Thus the unbeliever's argument will always presuppose

God because the unbeliever cannot supply the prior elementary conditions for the nonphysical laws of logic and morality. The triune God is the preexisting foundation for all debate. Deny God and one cannot account for debate.

> Therefore let all the house of Israel *know assuredly* that God has made this Jesus whom you crucified, both Lord and Christ (Acts 2:36 italic's mine).

A Good and Precious Gift

The Christian is to obey the law of God out of gratitude and love. We are to press that same law on the nonbeliever to demonstrate their need for the Savior. The law is good, and we are to delight in it. It is a good and precious gift from the Father of lights. If the triune God did not exist, then there is nothing special about the life of a human being. Human life is sacred and humanity has dignity inasmuch as mankind has been created in the image of God. Deny God, and there is nothing transcendent, or special about human life. Deny the triune God, and there is no moral difference in swatting a fly or pulling a weed over murdering an innocent schoolgirl. Thank God that is wrong. He created man in His own image and He gave mankind the moral law. We can justify absolute moral standards based on that very law. It is impossible for absolute, universal, and binding moral laws not to exist. Hence its impossible for the triune God not to exist. Therefore to argue against the existence of God and His issuing moral laws is like Benjamin Franklin's quip: "He who spits against the wind spits in his own face." If there are no ethical standards then I have no obligation nor does anyone else to correctly listen to anything the atheist says, including that there is no God. Thus he gets it right back in the face if he denies God and His moral law.

> But we know that the law is good if one uses it lawfully (1 Timothy 1:8).

110

CHAPTER 7
THE IMBECILITY OF GODLESS MORALS

The Self-Refuting Nature of Modern Ethics

"Your own wickedness will correct you, and your backslidings will rebuke you. Know therefore and see that it is an evil and bitter thing that you have forsaken the LORD your God, and the fear of Me is not in you," says the Lord GOD of hosts (Jeremiah 2:19).

Why I came here I know not... Why should I be anxious about an atom? (Byron).

The definition of a self-refuting statement: a universal statement that is not based on God's word and self-destructs on its own proposition because it is a statement that invalidates itself. It is self-contradictory. If the statement is true, then it must be false. A self-refuting statement is self-defeating and self-invalidating. It nullifies itself. The imbecility of it is that it cannot be true, for as much as it is true, then it is false.

The Self-Deceived Assert Self-Refuting Statements

A self-refuting statement fails to satisfy its own premise. It is necessarily false. If it is true, then it is false; if it is not true, it is false. Consequently it cannot be true. People want to be self-

111

deceived and will assert contradictory statements to avoid the truth found in Christ. Skepticism and every non-Christian assertion will always self-destruct. What they attempt to justify confutes itself. If you will be rational, you must be a Christian to account for the preconditions of the intelligibility of reason. We do not have to go around refuting every infidel's errant proposition. It will refute itself and is destroyed by its own credentials. If their proposition contradicts the Bible, it commits philosophical suicide. There are internal inconsistencies in all non-Christian systems of moral philosophy and thought. They are riddled with self-contradictions. And they are self-defeating and self-voiding. The Christian faith has total certainty, and we must demonstrate that the unbeliever has total uncertainty. Any notion that is contrary to Biblical thought is false.

The following is a short list (the full list can be found in my book: *God Does Exist!*) of self-refuting propositions is given to demonstrate the gaping defects that all non-Christian moral thought is intrinsically bound. Self-nullifying statements fail to satisfy their own premise. They are necessarily false. Below I record a number of self-refuting assertions. The self-refuting statement is written first and is followed by the stultifying question or appropriate response.

It is forbidden to forbid.
Do you forbid that which is forbidden?
You can't know anything for sure.
Are you sure of that?
There is no certainty.
Are you certain of that?
You can't know anything.
Do you know that?
I can't believe in anything that I can't see or feel.
Can you see or feel the point of that statement?
All knowledge begins with experience.
Did you experience that?
God is indescribable.

Is that your description of God?
Everything is just an illusion.
Then that statement is an illusion, so it is false, thus, all things are not illusions.
I believe only in science and the scientific method.
Is that statement scientifically testable?
True knowledge is only that knowledge that can be empirically verified.
Can you empirically verify that statement?
Reality is not fixed, hard, and foundational.
Is that statement fixed, hard, and foundational?
Moral truth depends on your experience.
Did you experience that proposition? No. Therefore it is false on its own terms.
Here, we have no rules.
Is that your rule?
We can only discover truth by testing and experimentation.
Are you able to test that assertion?
Apart from mathematics, we can know nothing for sure.
Is that proposition a mathematical equation? No. Then you are providing in what you say, the very basis to reject what you say.
I doubt everything.
If you tried to doubt everything, you would be clipping off the rope you're holding onto because the notion of doubting, itself, presupposes certainty.
Nobody's right.
Are you right?
Every attempt to fashion an absolute philosophy of truth and right is a delusion.
Is that true and right?

Modern Moral Values: The Problems

> One thing that does not change: The perceptual
> struggle of good and evil (T.S. Eliot).

A Las Vegas newspaper reported on the trouble with modern values as it lamented: "Janet Jackson's 'wardrobe malfunction,' Nicolette Sheridan's towel malfunction and her naked leap into the arms of Philadelphia Eagles wide receiver Terrell Owens in a promotion before ABC's 'Monday Night Football,' and the recent Detroit Pistons - Indiana Pacers game melee are just the most recent signs of a new culture that has emerged among Americans, and it's just the tip of the iceberg. Years ago, the lowest of lowdown men wouldn't use the kind of language that's routinely used today especially in the presence of women. To see men sitting while a woman was standing on a public conveyance used to be unthinkable. Children addressing adults by their first name was also against cultural norms, not to mention the use of foul language in the presence of or to adults. How about guys and girls walking down the street while the guy has his hand in the girl's rear pocket? The importance of customs, traditions and moral values as a means of regulating behavior is one motivation for people to behave themselves even if nobody's watching. Customs, traditions and moral values have been discarded without an appreciation for the role they played in creating a civilized society, and now we're paying the price. What's worse is that instead of a return to what worked, many people fail to make the connection and insist 'there ought to be a law.' As such it points to another failure of the so-called 'great generation' - the failure to transmit to their children what their parents transmitted to them."

It has been rare to set my eyes on a big city newspaper asserting and bewailing the fact that modern morals are weak. The author was correct in bemoaning the plight of the basic ethical structure of our culture. If you do not agree that this is troubling, I dare you to turn on *MTV* for five minutes and watch in horror as the Gangsta-rappers lead our nation's young people to their nefarious ethics. The moral trends, in much of our modern society, are aggressive, public embracing of indecencies. The basic values of the past generation are being supplanted by the vile and the vain.

> For all have sinned and fall short of the glory of
> God (Romans 3:23).

Oppression is not the Solution

One possible answer to the moral erosion is Islamic law. But this is unacceptable. A Christian magazine noted that "A 1,400-year-old Islamic system of family and business law that was approved without public fanfare in Ontario in October 2003 is now under review by the province's government. After several women's and human-rights' groups decried Ontario's use of Shari'ah law, which they say can be unfair and dangerous to women and children, the province's Ministry of the Attorney General ordered a review of the Arbitration Act. The 1991 legislation enables independent tribunals from various religions to arbitrate matters of family and business law according to their beliefs and customs. The shame and shunning a Muslim woman who 'goes against the flow' faces from her own family and community is so great that most of them don't want to risk losing everything that's important and will often stay in abusive, controlling relationships because of this,' Arjoman said. She cites the situation of one woman in her caseload who, since the introduction of the Shari'ah arbitration board, was divorced by her husband because she couldn't have sex with him. The woman who is in the advanced stages of cancer, was declared divorced and thrown out of the house along with her six children in the middle of the night. Her husband married another woman three days later and now has custody of the couple's six children, while his former wife is dying in a Toronto hospital."[53] Islamic law is oppressive and immoral and God's law rejects it.

Can science supply the foundation for moral values? Atheistic philosopher Bertrand Russell admitted: "Science has nothing to say about 'values.' This I admit."[54] Science cannot provide the fixed absolute foundation necessary for moral laws. And much of Western science has embraced a version of evolution and the survival of the fittest. This damning doctrine not only fails to supply ethics, it asserts that the killing of the weak is a good thing for the promotion of a stronger species. Russell was right. Science cannot provide absolute moral values and we must go further than agreeing to that. Science must have moral laws under it and over it or it will fall into more and more hoaxes and frauds. Those who push evolutionary ethics will not get a free ride. Judgment will come to them and all who do not trust the Savior. The great Ralph Venning rightly asserted that "God will take vengeance and is righteous in doing so."

An Omnipotent Lord is Needed

We must follow Jesus Christ in our ethical pursuit. We should care and have compassion on others, even if their genes will weaken the gene pool. Bennett aimed well when he said, "One temptation, the very modern temptation, is not to care, or at least to pretend not to care..."[55] He then offers us this clear rejection of selfish aimed, survival of the fittest, ethics: "That sin is a burden and a bondage is nowhere more apparent than in intemperate (lack of self control), in that obsession of selfish, self preservation, which seeks itself in vain."[56] When someone asked St. Augustine whether he might tell a lie for his neighbor's good "Oh no," he said, "You must not tell a lie to save the world."

The Moral Sense

James Q. Wilson in his book, *The Moral Sense*, argues correctly that, "There is in human nature the elements of a natural moral sense... a huge body of evidence from a variety of disciplines including animal behavior, anthropology, evolutionary theory, biology, brain science, genetics, primatology, education, and psychology."[57] Wilson is incorrect in asserting that it is innately biological rather than spiritual (Romans chapter one). He marshals a wide range of empirical research over the last fifty years. He drives the point home, page after page, that man has an inborn desire for moral values. He then admits: "If modern man had taken seriously the main intellectual currents of the last century or so, he would have found himself confronted by the need to make moral choices where the very possibility of making such choices had been denied... As a result, man is adrift on an uncharted sea, left to find his moral bearings without a compass... and able to do little more than utter personal preferences..."[58] Wilson then sums up his mutable moral values: "Mankind's moral sense is not a strong beacon light, radiating outward to illuminate in sharp outline all that it touches. It is, rather, a small candle flame, casting shadows, flickering, and sputtering in the strong winds of power and passion, greed and ideology."[59]

This is the only ethical value system that can remain when one believes in the theory of evolution. Macro-evolution argues that the universe is the product of blind chance, it has no intrinsic end or purpose. We are just skipping on a small spinning blue ball until it melts into the background radiation at the inevitable coming cosmic eternal heat-death. To do this we must ignore all design, engineering, beauty, and the finely tuned cosmic orbits.

The late evolutionist, Stephen J. Gould once proposed that the Panda's clumsy thumb was proof against a designer God. The Panda's thumb "wins no prize in an engineer's derby." God would not be a bumbling engineer, thus God did not design the Panda and the universe. Yet if one takes the time to study the Panda, one quickly discovers that the Panda's thumb makes a great bamboo peeler, the Panda's primary food. His thumb is quite workable for his food and survival, but not for running your cell phone or Blackberry. Thus the Panda cannot play checkers or program your DVD player. But the Panda eats very well. Yes, God is the designer and the engineer. Evolutionists have to go back to the drawing board and tell us how chance acting on matter can engineer anything.

The New Ethics are not Ethical

Before Darwin almost everyone in the West believed in a universal moral order that transcends man and that makes demands on us. Now many have a new ethic: the gay movement, the trans-gender advocates, man-boy clubs, and polygamy. Men have fought for a culture that would not be based on divine authority, but in the authority of self. A lot of this came from the European philosopher, Rousseau, who pleaded for a morality that is based on "inner freedom." The problem with that dictum is men can have the desire to blow up women and children and feel inner freedom. Some could have that heart-felt liberty in murder, rape, illegal dumping of mass pollution, and all manner of evil. There must be a law that transcends our human heart. For our hearts are sinful and dark and they are not omniscient and omnipotent. Omniscience and omnipotence are required to make any absolute indubitable law. This leaves God alone to make immutable moral laws.

The biggest obstacle for certain ethics is Rousseau's notion that men are basically good. Liberals follow Rousseau's moral philosophy. They dismiss evil and wickedness as myth and righteousness and holiness as oppressive. Christians have a low view of man and a high view of God. We hold to the great expectation of what God can do to the human heart and civil culture through Christ reigning in the people of God. All men have what Rabbinic literature describes as *yatzu ha ra* and *yatzu ha tov:* the dual propensity to do bad or good. Even evil men usually care for their own family. Mob bosses send a dozen roses to drape the coffin of the wise guy they just gunned down. But civil government must put in place law with checks and balances to limit wickedness and chaos. The unbridled evil, that unrestrained men would do if they were allowed, must be held in check. Knowing the warped nature of humanity, people must have a government that reflects diversity in unity. A congress, a judicial branch, and an executive branch. A wise people should not allow a dictator to hold all civil authority. A government that reflects God's nature, the Trinity (diversity in unity), helps suppress man's lower and base impulses.

Man is not the Standard

Our epistemological means of discerning what is good and right is found in the Bible. That is our authority and our guide. Man is not the standard. Reason is not the standard. Pragmatism is not the standard. And utilitarianism is not the standard. Why? Because only the Bible can provide a standard based on an all-knowing and unchanging being, God. The standard must be based on an immutable and omniscient source or ethics could change. Only an all-knowing being could make laws that should be universally applied to all men at all times. If moral laws were based on finite humanity: lying and murder could be good. This is impossible and collapses the shelf that it sits on. If lying could be good, there can be no truth, which is a truth claim. This is self-refuting.

We are ruled by a sovereign God who gives us laws and proscriptions that do not change because He cannot change. There is no place for autonomy. Nietzsche and Hitler proclaimed an ethic based on autonomy and survival of the fittest. Their values led to the deaths of millions. If a philosopher, judge, or politician try to dismiss God from ethics, they end up with mass graves. Liberty is not autonomy. Liberty is freedom to be who you are and what you want to be within the values of God's word.

Without Biblical restrictions from an unchanging God, injustice would flourish. To have good people, a nation must have a moral code from an unchanging and all-knowing God. Only He can provide an unchanging standard of good since He alone is unchanging.

A Heart Inclined Toward God

A culture is good if it has laws that correspond to God's law and the people obey them. The general equity of the commandments of God must be the foundation to establish civil law. The civil law cannot touch the inward heart of the citizens. It can restrain those with inward evil from harming their neighbor and their community. All citizens should drive the speed limit, bear true witness in court, and respect the property of others. The believer should also inwardly desire to drive the speed limit, be truthful and respectful. The believer is born again, hence has a heart inclined toward God. Thus all men must obey the law outwardly and the Christian obeys the law outwardly and inwardly. The desire of the unbeliever is to speed, but he is restrained by the police car on the roadside. The believer is tempted, but is restrained inwardly by the Holy Spirit. And when the Christian sins, he feels bad and asks for forgiveness and repents. Christians do struggle, but God is greater than our heart and He matures us into obedient followers.

The laws of the Bible must be the "final court of appeal for ethics." Biblical ethics are not to be only "descriptive of human behavior, but prescriptive (deontological: that which is obligatory) in discerning the will of God" in real-life situations and specific actions that are based on its general principals. Thus all individuals and nations must affirm and embrace the commandments of God in erecting laws and in living their lives.

What Is Your Standard?

Below I recall a conversation on ethics I had with a skeptic:

> *Skeptic:* Well, I don't believe in the Bible. I only believe in doing what is loving.
>
> *Christian:* Ok. How do you define what is loving? What is your standard that defines the loving action in a given situation?
>
> *Skeptic:* My heart. My feelings give me the way to love someone.
>
> *Christian:* How should other people discern the proper, loving, ethical action?
>
> *Skeptic*: By their feelings. What their heart tells them is right and loving.
>
> *Christian:* What if someone's heart tells him to rape a baby or harm the environment? He claims it's the loving thing to do.
>
> *Skeptic:* That's wrong. That's not loving.
>
> *Christian:* By what standard do you make that assessment?
>
> *Skeptic:* Me. My feelings.
>
> *Christian:* The problem with your ethical system is it cannot bind others to a fixed, ethical standard. Without that, anyone can do anything evil, and call it loving if they *feel* it's OK.

There must be an unchanging standard of absolute moral laws. Personal preference ethics cannot condemn Nazism, slavery, abuse, environmental destruction, murder, and rape. It is false and against God's word. There are moral absolutes and God has revealed them in the Bible. When I was in public school, teachers taught me situational ethics. They would employ extreme hypothetical situations to force the students to choose the lesser of two evils. They did this to try to shake their pupils out of the belief in an absolute moral law. They would propose the dilemma: If you are only able to save one child from an oncoming train that was headed for the tracks that your sister and her friend were stuck on, which one would you pull to safety? Or, if you had to tell a lie to hide an innocent man from certain death from some storm troopers, would you? A couple truths the situational ethics proponents usually forget: God is sovereign and God answers prayer. If one is stuck in an ethical dilemma, the sovereign God has placed him there, and he can pray to God and God can deliver him. Many might claim that's a simple-minded answer. Yes it might be, but God is God and He answers prayer. I'll trust Him over my own wisdom.

Honesty is Essential

Our epistemological means of discerning what is good and right is found in the Bible. That is our authority and our guide. Man is not the standard. Science is not the standard. Why? Because only the Bible can provide a standard based on an all-knowing and unchanging being, God. The standard must be based on an unchanging source, or ethics could change. If moral standards were mutable this would mean: lying and murder on one day are bad. The next day they might be good. This is impossible and collapses the floor it stands on. If lying could be good, there can be no truth, which is a truth claim. This is self-confounding. Honesty is not just the best policy, it must be practiced in order to communicate and live with others. William Bennett reminds us: "Society cannot exist or function properly when people aren't honest."[60] He then reminds us that "Our forefathers understood that honesty is essential to life, liberty, and the pursuit of happiness and are impossible without the honesty of our country's citizens... Honesty... involves consistency between our thoughts and our actions."[61] But what survival value would honesty be for natural selection to infuse this into our genes? One must presuppose honesty to account for communication, but evolutionary advantage would be with those who lie for personal gain and survival. Deception and dishonesty would better insure the multiplication of more of their genes.

We are superintended by the hand of a sovereign God who gives us laws and principals that do not change because He is immutable. There is no place for full and free personal autonomy apart from God. Nietzschian philosophy, communism, and Nazism proclaim an ethic based on autonomy and survival of the fittest. Their foundational values led to the murder of tens of millions. If a man attempts to dismiss God from ethics, they end up with concentration camps and genocide. Without Biblical restrictions from an unchanging God, wickedness would flourish. To have a righteous nation, it must have a moral code from an unchanging and inerrant God. Only He could provide a fixed standard of good.

A Huge Question

The major question a nonbeliever must ask is: Why should nations outlaw atrocities and wickedness? Let natural selection alone, and have the fittest kill, strive, and survive. The presuppositions of evolution cannot contend that killing weaker members of the gene pool is morally wrong. Consistent Darwinism demands that the stout, healthy and vital kill off the genetically defective and weaker members of the biological group to allow the best genes to multiply and the weak genes to disappear. The elderly, the mentally unfit, and handicapped should be killed off so their genetic make-up will not pollute the gene pool. The weak should just be used and harvested for utilitarian goals for the betterment of the whole species. The prohibitions against rape and murder of the physiological defective are inconsistent with Darwinism, yet consistent with Christianity. Evolutionists cannot supply justifications for any of the Ten Commandments, including murder and rape. Christianity does and must be true because it alone provides the preexisting rational and spiritual environment needed for unchanging ethical standards.

An evolutionary atheist has no universal, inerrant, immutable, invariant, all-knowing source for universal and immutable moral laws. Christianity has given man the prior essential conditions for objective and unchanging moral laws. One who believes in a random, chaotic, self-organized biochemical that evolved into Einstein and Edison cannot justify objective absolute ethical precepts. Any atheist who claims that murder or rape is always wrong is an ethical crypto-Christian. He must borrow from the Christian view of life and morals. If one gives up God, he must also give up moral law and the identification of evil. He cannot justify any assertion that something is evil without stealing his ethics from Christianity. If something is always evil, then there are absolutes. If there are absolutes, and there must be, then the God of the Bible must live and has spoken.

Exquisitely Designed

Time magazine ran a front page spread on the scientific theory of Intelligent Design in August of 2005. The article reported that a Harris poll found that 55 percent of adults surveyed said children should be taught Creationism and ID (Intelligent Design) in public schools. The article argued that there are no real holes in Darwin's theory. But admitted that, "...living things are simply too exquisitely complex to have evolved by a combination of chance mutations and natural selection... that living organisms contain such ingenious structures as the eye and systems like the mechanism for clotting blood, which contains at least 20 interacting proteins." This is irreducibly complex because "removing or altering any part invalidates the whole... they could not have arisen through gradual fits and starts of evolution..."[62] Of course the problem with Darwinian evolutionary theory: It is impossible because it cannot supply the foundational epistemological guarantee. Christianity alone does. In the same article in *Time,* Christian scientist Francis Collins fawned over science: "For me scientific discovery is also an occasion of worship."[63] Skeptic Steven Pinker revealing his intellectual pre-committment charged, "Our own bodies are riddled with quirks that no competent engineer would have planned... goose bumps that uselessly try to warm us by fluffing up long-gone fur."[64] Well I do have some hairy friends that get goose bumps when they experience something lovely, transcendent, deep or touching, without ever getting cold. This is not the Christian argument and Pinker's contention is just as weak. How does his theory provide pre-intellectual starting points to even propose his theory? He cannot. Only Christian theism can.

Pinker rambles on: "The moral design of nature is as bungled as its engineering design. What twisted sadist would have invented a parasite that blinds millions of people... If an intelligent designer lived on Earth, people would break his windows."[65] Pinker and almost all atheistic Darwinians are blind to their own philosophical predispositions. He presupposes that there wasn't an Adamic Fall. He pre-commits to a rejection of sin entering the world and infusing error, pain, and brokeness throughout the creation. Christians presuppose the Fall and with it came trouble, destruction, and parasites. One of the main problems Pinker must face is the difficulty of not being able to account for morality. He can supply no unchanging source of moral law. Thus when he speaks of what is moral he presupposes God without understanding his dilemma.

Questions Evolution Cannot Answer

The following is a list of a few simple questions that the theory of evolution cannot provide any logical reply:

> How did the human eye, capable of performing ten billion calculations per second, evolve by chance?

How do lifeless chemicals come alive?

What is the evolutionary advantage of an organism having a half-wing on its way to a full wing? Would not the extra weight, of the less than fully formed wing, and the potential clumsiness of the useless appendage, lower the chance of survival and not enhance it?

How did warm-blooded birds evolve from cold-blooded reptiles?

Does the doctrine of the survival of the fittest assert that the organisms that produce the greatest number of surviving offspring are the most fit? If so, why would a cockroach or bacteria ever ascend, and eventually evolve into large body-mass organisms that are extremely susceptible to extinction, and produce much fewer offspring? Do the simple organisms of bugs and bacteria need to evolve?

Can information, such as the DNA code, come from non-intelligence? Is there anywhere, where we observe non-intelligence producing information?

Can chance plus time plus agitation produce information? (Try putting a pencil and paper in an empty cement mixer and turn it on high. You can check it every day and after a hundred years you will still not get poetry or even one sentence through chance plus energy plus time acting on matter).

Is it because science cannot supply the conditions

for morality that it is prone to fakes, forgeries, and frauds? Many of these frauds have been exposed in medical and scientific studies. The investigators discovered that the dishonest scientists were seeking grant money which motivated them to lie about their medical research. This dishonest research (falsifying medical and drugs tests, the Piltdown man hoax, the January 2000 Archaeoraptor fake promoted by *National Geographic* magazine, and other projects) is very harmful. Why is there such a long history of scientific hoaxes and fraud?

Deny God, and affirm evolutionary materialism, and you undermine morality. Nature offers scores of "inhumane" conduct. Are humans to follow the animals that kidnap and force females to have sex with them? Should we act like praying mantises and black widows that devour their males? One finds a plethora of beastly killings, forced intercourse, and voids of egalitarianism in nature. Monogamy, self-sacrifice, and enduring love are missing in most of the animal kingdom. Without God, there is no reason mankind should not practice the same brutality.

The Brain and the Mind

The physicalist atheist asserts that the mind is the physical brain. The human brain lacks any nonphysical actions taking place within its boundaries. But if the human mind consisted only of hard chemicals and neurons bouncing around in the skull, human thoughts would be no more true or valued than an afternoon tamale food-belch. Both are just chemical reactions. This means that there is no rational reason to count my thoughts more important than a burp; they are just meaningless and empty chemical reactions. This of course is self-voiding. If my thoughts and words are meaningless, then they are not true; hence my thoughts cannot be meaningless. My thoughts are not just concrete chemical reactions.

The University of California, Irvine issued a report based on planting false memories. Researchers were able to persuade 131 students that they liked food as a child that they presently dislike and vice-versa. Test subjects were told that sometime in their childhood strawberry ice cream made them ill. They told the students to amplify that false memory and describe where they were and who had witnessed them getting sick. After the study 41 percent of those tested responded that they would no longer eat strawberry ice cream. They were able to reverse the subjects taste by planting false memories of food that the test subjects first did not like (asparagus) and after the study they now craved and wanted to enjoy that which they formerly disliked. The researchers described the results as mind-over-matter. The power of suggestion can change our cravings because our minds transcend our brains.

The Brain, the Mind, and a Computer

Research into harnessing brain signals by Dr. Jonathan Wolpaw revealed some startling results after 20 years of study. The technology demonstrated that the mind can control a computer when the brain has tiny electrodes placed on the surface of the brain. The people had a chip 1/25 of an inch inserted on the brain and the determined thoughts of the mind could move a cursor around the screen. The mind moved it without any stimulation of the brain. Therefore that research supplied proof that the mind is distinct from the hard tissue brain.

A mind, distinct from the brain, destroys the theory of evolution. Evolution materialists do not believe mankind has a spirit. His soul is only "a little wind and smoke." Research on the brain can lead to the conclusion that the mind alone is independent of the brain. Some legitimate science has uncovered reasons to believe that life survives the physical death. A Yale University professor (using scientific theory alone) wrote that he would "bet yes" that the afterlife is a fact. When one submits to God's revelation, there is no betting. It is impossible for God, and the afterlife that He reveals, not to exist. To ask the question about a possible afterlife presupposes that God lives, and His word is true. When the atheist backs up in a conversation and says, "Hold on, I'm searching for a word," point out the inconsistency. I like to ask them: "Who is searching?" Those who claim that only the physical world exists, and that their mind is just a block of flesh, can't answer that question. Frequently, they will quickly see their dilemma. Thomas Huxley, in one of his moments of weakness, asked, "How is it that anything so remarkable as the state of consciousness comes about as a result of irritating nervous tissue, is it just as unaccountable as the appearance of the Djinn, when Aladdin rubbed his lamp?"

The Mind is not Identical with the Brain

Philosopher Dallas Willard in *Christianity Today*, November 18, 2002, posits: "Clearly there is in human beings a profoundly important connection between the states and events of the brain and those of personal existence. But the person is not identical with the brain (or the DNA or the body as a whole). Why? Because there are thousands upon thousands of truths about the person that are not truths about the body. And there are many *kinds* of truths about persons that are not the *kinds* of truths that apply to the body or any part thereof. Inspect the brain in any way you will; you will not find these truths or even know that they exist from what you do find there. Gottfried Wilhelm Leibniz pointed this out a long time ago, and no satisfactory way around it has ever been found. The brain... is one part of the embodied dimension of the human person."

Additional research has demonstrated that there is a distinction between the mind and the brain. One study had brain surgeons open up the skulls of brain surgery patients to expose their gray matter. The researchers then electrically stimulated the area of the brain that lifts the right arm. They stimulated it, and the arm lifted without the patient's permission. Then the scientists instructed their patients to resist the lifting of the arm when they stimulated the same spot in the brain. They stimulated that area, and all the patients could resist the lifting of their arm. This proved that the mind can control the brain. Another study, conducted by U.C.L.A., had doctors give depressed patients two sets of pills. One was an antidepressant medicine, and the other was a placebo pill. Both groups said they experienced relief of symptoms: 52 percent of those who received the medication, and 38 percent of those who received the sugar pill. The interesting thing was the discovery that the brain waves, of the placebo-taking patients, acutely changed after taking the fake pill. Their brain chemistry and brain waves were altered without any medication, merely from their own "minds." The mind controls the gray matter and can change it; the mind is distinct from the brain. The researchers reported that they were "stunned" because there were actual "hardware" changes in the brain, by the power of suggestion. The power of suggestion comes from the mind working the brain. The mind can change and "alter" how the brain works. This is clear evidence that the mind moved the brain and is distinct from the brain tissue.

How Tyranny Begins

Emerson had it right when he mused, "All ages of belief have been great; all of unbelief have been mean." This full scale national philosophical embrace of evolutionary theory by the Nazi's (14 million murdered through the underpinnings of evolution) and the Soviets (atheist Stalin applying evolutionary theory by murdering 30-60 million), and Mao's China (stou atheist Mao mass murdering 25-40 million in his embrace of evolution) resulted in many times the mass murder than all the religious wars and crime combined. "The purpose of moral law is to prevent the strong always having their way," Ovid observed. Look at the numbers: Murder in the name of religion is absolutely dwarfed by the evolutionists. Do not ever accept the notion that religion has killed more people than anything else. That is a huge lie. And remember Jesus taught love and not hate. He commanded His followers not to murder and not to kill in His name, but to love your enemies. Thus those who kill in His name are not His followers by definition. I can stride into the ocean water and claim I'm a killer whale. But once a shark bites my leg off, it becomes painfully obvious that my claim doesn't make it so. Therefore one who claims to follow the loving Prince of Peace and kills in His name is not a real Christian.

Absolutes We Must Have to Know Anything

We need moral law. As John Locke noted, "Wherever law ends, tyranny begins." As we discovered earlier, no other worldview or religion can provide the necessary *a priori* conditions for universal moral absolutes. Some tribes in Calabar murder twin babies because they believe that twins are cursed. In some villages it is was the tribal law to kill the slaves and wives of the survivors of a household when a rich man died. Many other cruel customs and laws have been erected by morally blind men. God has blessed us with a clear, unchanging, universal, and compassionate law that forbids murder, rape, robbery, and all manner of wickedness. This is not just a "deeply held view." It is the pre-commitment that alone gives us the absolutes we must have to know anything at all, including moral truth. I am certain that it is always wrong to rape women and to sexually abuse children. I am certain because God, who knows all things and holds all power, has revealed it to men. Nuance and relativism cannot fog up that clarity. The contrary to ethical absolutes is self-impaling and it is impossible for the God of the Bible not to exist. Reality is unequivocal in its declaration that God lives.

Atheism has to deal with more than a moral enigma. To rationally justify the supposition that there is no God, anywhere, one would have to possess universal and infinite knowledge. Only God has complete and infinite knowledge. Therefore one who annunciates that there is no God, would himself have to have complete and infinite knowledge. This would make him God. This is absurd. Hence atheism is false.

The Darwinian worldview not only commits philosophical suicide, it brings despair that grows in its claimants. The unbeliever Byron screams in horror on his death bed as he hollers in delusion that his bedspread is on fire. Voltaire rants and raves about being cursed and forsaken and damned for his rejection of Christ during his last days. We have been spared the horrible last words of the bombastic atheist Madalyn Murray O'Hair when her atheist partner murdered her and her atheistic grandchildren for some cash. Yet her final utterances must have been filled with anguish. A man in London heard a lecture on anti-theism and socialism. He went home and wrote that the Bible was the greatest possible deception. Then he shot himself. Without God and His love and law, man has no purpose and falls into depression and despair. This leads to horror in death and eternity.

Virtue Sought

Moral values seem to be somehow outside the scientific realm.

Virtue must be sought after again in our culture. A virtue is good if it has laws that correspond to God's law. The general equity of the commandments of God must be the foundation to erect civil law. The civil law cannot touch the inward heart of the citizens. It can restrain those with inward evil from harming their neighbor and their community, but it cannot change one's wicked heart. All citizens should drive sober, render honest testimony in court, and respect the property of his fellow man. The believer should also have a heartfelt desire to drive to obey civil law and be honest and respectful. But why should an atheist care if babies and women are murdered and tortured? When a killer pours acid or burns them alive, if there is no God, then the tortured person is just a meaningless makeup of molecules that are only recombined and rearranged. If the triune God does not exist, there is no possibility of good, value, ethics, right, or justice. We are just hyped-up organized molecules in Levi's. Deny God and the existentialist pagan Sartre asked the right question: "Why not commit suicide?" Without God and His moral law there is no injustice or purpose, only despair.

Ethics have to come from a transcendent and all-knowing source. As one apologist contended: "The moral law is a real thing that is independent of us, not something that is made up by us." Only an omnipresent and omnipotent Lord can supply the required prior conditions for moral law. God has done this and we must affirm it and live it. The law teaches us that we are sinners in need of a Savior. Jesus is that Savior and you must trust in Him and His atonement and resurrection. The law also instructs us how to govern ourselves and how to live as individuals. And the law of God provides the foundation for civil law. Yes, unless we begin by presupposing that God lives and God has spoken, we have no rational basis for knowing anything. Objective and all-applying moral laws are a philosophical essential. But God, morals, and truth get very personal. Trouble comes. Pain and difficulties arrive. But God is very close and consoling, and He is the most important being in your life.

Jesus is the Risen Lord

Jesus Christ rose from the dead and unless Christianity is true, we can know nothing of reality. If we can know nothing of reality, we cannot know that proposition. Unless the God of revelation is and has spoken, human knowledge has no intelligible basis and there cannot be moral absolutes or laws of logic. Thus the contrary of Christianity is impossible. The risen reigning Christ is our source of morals. He is alive. If you came to a fork in a road and on one side of the fork was a dead man and on the other side there was a live person standing, who would you ask for directions? Not only would you ask the living man, it is certain that you could only ask the living man. And Jesus is the only founder of a religion that rose from the dead. He is the only one who promised a resurrection, and He kept His promise. You can visit the tombs of all the deceased religious leaders and find their remains still in the grave. You can visit their occupied graves just as you can the heterodox leaders: David Koresh, Joseph Smith, and Muhammad. All these allotheists died and stayed dead; their occupied sarcophaguses attest to this. However Jesus rose from the dead as promised. His grave is empty.

Jesus proclaimed, "All power on earth and heaven has been given to me." No force could keep Him down. The Romans killed Him. He was put into a cave tomb, and a huge boulder was rolled at a downward angle in front of the cave. Then they pasted Caesar's seal on the crypt, and posted Roman guards to protect the tomb. Ancient hostile Jewish and pagan sources all report that the grave of Christ is empty. Not one ancient historical source denies the empty tomb. And all Christ's followers died believing that they saw Him risen from the dead. They did not recant even upon brutal torture and death.

Men do not die for a lie willingly, if they know they have been deceived. The followers of Jim Jones, the people who discovered that he was a kook and a fraud, tried to escape Jonestown. Once they knew Jones was an impostor, and that he whipped up a batch of poison Kool-Aid, they ran and hid in the jungle. Many others tried to escape and were shot. They knew Jones was a charlatan and they did not want to die for him. However the Apostles and hundreds of others in the first century died for Jesus because they knew Jesus was alive. Remember the craze of Elvis sightings in the late 1980's? Elvis was very popula and beloved by millions and he suddenly died in 1977. About ten years later rumors circulated around the country of Elvis spottings. Gail Giorgio wrote a book, *Is Elvis Alive?*, contending that Elvis never died and was alive. His evidence he offered was the grave stone on Presley's grave misspelled his middle name as Aaron and not Aron. The other evidence he presented was Elvis' mother died at age 46 but it could have been at age 42. Thus Elvis would fake his own death at age 42. Another unconvincing proof was the fact that Presley's father did not want to receive the flag from the military at the funeral of Elvis. The evidence of the resurrection of Jesus goes way beyond this thin theory by Giorgio. And no one in Hawaii claimed to see Elvis walking on Wikiki Beach and was ready to die for that claim. Elvis is dead and stayed dead. Jesus is risen and alive.

The first-century followers of Christ died believing that He was perfectly and absolutely sinless. Many followers spent day and night with Him for over three years. And they believed He was without sin. If you spent sixty minutes with any other human, you would soon find out that they were not perfect. You would not lay down your life, declaring that they were sinless. You would not die for what you know is a lie. Christ had all His friends and enemies confess that He did not sin. The disciples, His betrayer, His religious enemies, and His Roman enemies, were all in agreement on one subject: Jesus never sinned. No one could accuse Jesus of sin. Jesus is alive as the perfect sinless Messiah; that is a fact. It is not a brute fact that stands by itself and awaits the judgment of autonomous reason, but it is true, and it is impossible for it not to be true. Since Jesus is risen and perfect, He is our moral example and we are to obey His words because He is Lord.

Contradictions and Errors?

Many skeptics charge that the Bible has mistakes and records reports that contradict one another. Most of these alleged errors are cleared up when one studies a little deeper than the surface level that Jesus Seminar devotees chip at. One should note, in the New Testament, the writers utilize at least three different calendars (the Roman, Judean, and Galilean) and at least two different methods of telling the time (Jewish and Pagan). This solves a host of the claimed contradictions. Another notion one must understand prior to looking at the text is an argument from silence doesn't offer any positive evidence. One Gospel writer could record a slap in the face and the other Gospel writer doesn't include the slap. This is not a contradiction. In any two eyewitness reports there can be facts not noted because the witness did not think it was necessary. This doesn't mean the event did not happen. Most of the rest of the supposed questions can be answered through better study of the Biblical Greek and Hebrew. Certain nuances can be better discerned when the astute student puts on the correct linguistic and cultural lens when he researches the documents.

I have studied about a hundred alleged errors and contradictions in scripture. Most were easily dismissed and all the others were solved as I dug in a little deeper. One time my preteen daughter watched a TV show. The skeptical host interviewed a liberal scholar who contended that the New Testament wasn't a hundred percent reliable. He stated that the Gospel writers record three different sets of last words from Jesus. Therefore there are errors. My daughter looked at me frazzled, puzzled, and melancholy as she sadly begged me, "How do we know what to believe in the Bible?" I told her not to fret. That she will hear many disbelievers argue that there are some mistakes in the Holy Bible. There are not any. It's God's word and without having an intellectual pre-commitment to it we cannot account for anything in the world. Without God revealing His infallible word we would not be able to make sense out of our experience. Only Christianity can provide the required preconditions for the intelligibility of our world. And in this purported contradiction recall that the Gospel writers never assert that these are the last words of Jesus on the cross. Never. Each book records some o the final words of Jesus, but they never teach us that they were the last words. Thus any of the words recorded near the end of the life of Jesus, may or may not have been His last exact words. The Bible only records different words that Jesus spoke near His death.

The Modern Rival Fails

Modernity's foundation for ethics is supplied by the theory of evolution. Macro-evolution is ateleological. It has no purpose. The universe is the product of blind chance, it has no real end or purpose. We are just squatting on a small spinning blue ball until it melts into the background radiation of the coming eternal burnout. Therefore nothing ultimately matters and morals are based on the survival of the fittest. Evolutionists reject the design of the cosmos and His moral law. They ignore the clear design, the biological engineering, and the finely tuned inner and outer worlds. They *believe* it just all happened by chance.

> In the beginning, God created the Heavens and the
> Earth (Genesis 1:1).

Recall Gould's assertion that the Giant Panda's clumsy thumb was proof against a designer. Yet the bear's thumb is quite workable for his food and survival, not for running your PC keyboard, or dialing your cell phone. The Panda cannot sew a new dress or play poker, but the Panda eats very well. Yes, God is the designer and He is a smart designer. The anti-design evolutionists have to go back to the drawing board and demonstrate how chance acting on matter can engineer anything.

Evolution is vanity considering that it cannot supply a right ethical standard. Many naturalists claim that one can discover ethics by natural law. Should we admire a bee that destroys its female offspring at birth? Should we highly esteem and imitate the male bear's morality? When they come upon a bear cub they attack it and try to eat the little live bear. Can we really find universal morality in nature? When a spider eats her mate, is that morally good? Observing good and bad in nature does not provide a fixed standard of good and bad. One cannot form ethics from the tooth and claw of nature. Survival of the fittest as the thrust of one's morality means: kill all the weak, take advantage of the women, and murder your competition. A Godless theory cannot supply the invariant universals necessary for fixed universal moral laws. Ungodly ideologies are arbitrary and necessarily false.

The theory of evolution is supported by arguments that are made up of premises that employ logic. Arguments require God. Evolution is modern man's "frenzied dream" to rinse God and righteousness out of the world. It swept through European academia like a big wheel through a tomato patch. Why? Because nonbelievers want complete freedom to sin and embrace sin and to live in the sinfulness of sin. History records that the first generation which embraced evolution went from the glee of high school prank giddiness to a dug in dogmatism. But why would a weed that is so stout and strong, so good at reproducing in my backyard evolve into a fish or a frog with the hassle of laying eggs and having to feed the young and all that messy stuff? Why? The weeds survive quite nicely even if I spray them with turbo weed killer: they always come back.

Highly regarded philosopher Willard Quine has noted that the falsification of a theory involves more that disproving its predication. Well, the true and living God reveals its actually easier than that, the reality is, all reason and predication are bound to the laws of logic and the laws of logic require an unchanging all knowing triune God. Evolution is just a theory with a false premise and a false conclusion.

Darwin railed against the Creator when he quipped to Lyell "Do you believe God designed the shape of my nose? If so, ' have nothing more to say." So Darwin's attempt to dismiss God with a jocular question, implying that God doesn't micromanage the creation, itself utilizes logic and thus is dependent upon the

God he tries to deny. Under Darwinian thought, Nazi's murdering millions is only wrong because the winners declared that Hitler was wrong. If a democratic nation passes laws that call for rounding up and murdering minorities, by what standard can a democratic atheist label this wrong? What if all nations pass similar laws and a huge majority believes that genocide and atrocities are good and proper? If one relies on a human standard, like democracy, all sorts of evil can be affirmed in voting and that would make it right. Many societies have murdered female babies because they valued males more. China is a recent example. Upon atheistic assumptions, one cannot have a standard that declares this to be morally wrong. Human preference cannot be the basis of morals because humanity is not perfect, transcendent, and immutable. Only God is.

You Reap What You Sow

The cosmos is under the providential control of God. It is bound by inviolable laws. Scientists have discovered these rules and designate them the laws of physics. Only the God of the Bible, a being who spoke the world into existence and sustains and upholds it, only that being is the necessary precondition for these laws. The sacred writings of all the worlds religions offer bizarre notions about the universe and how it operates. Without exception, these deities of other religions could not regulate and order the world. A God of provision and control is foreign to all the false religions. The Bible is absolutely accurate and God is the *a priori* essential needed to supply the foundations for the physical sciences. God's word teaches that our world is a planned and purposed creation by the God who designed it. The Bible outlines providence and induction: "God stretches out the north over empty space; He hangs the earth on nothing. He binds up the water in His thick clouds, yet the clouds are not broken under it. He covers the face of His throne, and spreads His cloud over it. He drew a circular horizon on the face of the waters, at the boundary of light and darkness" (Job 26:7-10). Scripture enunciates the sphere shape of the earth: "It is He who sits above the circle of the earth, and its inhabitants are like grasshoppers, who stretches out the heavens like a curtain, and spreads them out like a tent to dwell in" (Isaiah 40:22). The notion of the earth existing as a round globe hanging on nothing was unknown in the ancient world except here in the Bible.

> Do not be deceived, God is not mocked; for whatever a man sows, that he will also reap (Galatians 6:7).

God is not mocked. His holiness is immutable. His laws do not change. He is the indispensable source for induction and causality. Do not be deceived or led astray or deluded, you will reap what you sow. God is not mocked. The word "mocked" means: "to turn your nose up at." God is not made the fool. He is not mocked. If you plant corn, guess what comes up? Corn. In this world, you get what you plant. Only an all-powerful and all-knowing God could guarantee induction and provide the basis for the scientific method. Deny God and you have no justifiable reason to expect carrots when you plant carrot seeds. God is the required foundation for science.

Law/Gospel: Distinct But Not Separate

The predominant functions of the moral law and God's commandments:

    I.   Restrain Evil.
   II.   Reveal Sin/our Depravity.
  III.   Assist in our sanctification.

One must not confuse and commingle law and gospel: God's commands with God's promises. The law is not just the Old

Testament inasmuch as the Old Testament contains the gospel and the gospel is not just the New Testament for the New Testament contains law. The law accuses. The law commands and demands. It's what God expects out of His creatures in our thoughts, words and works. For it is not the ten recommendations, it is the Ten Commandments. It is rigorous. The law doesn't say just do the best you can. God does not grade on a curve. The final requires perfection or one does not enter heaven. It demands one hundred percent, every moment, in thought, word and deed. The good news is Christ has expiated the transgressions against the law for His sheep by grace through faith. The greatest good news is that Christ has made satisfaction for the sins, the mistakes, and the commandment breaking of His people.

The gospel has attained and acquired for all Christians, without any works or merit on our part, the forgiveness of sins and the imputed righteousness of Christ that avails before God and provides eternal life. The law is written on our hearts and the gospel comes from outside us from God's grace (Galatians 3:10-12). Scripture tells us the law is everything that demands perfect obedience to God and pronounces God's curses on all transgressors (Romans 3:19). The law of God renders all the world guilty before God's holiness and reveals the knowledge of sin (Romans 3:20-23). How can one avoid Hell? Jesus taught that it is very simple, "Be perfect as your Heavenly Father is perfect" (Matthew 5:48). Do that everyday and live. Recall what Jesus said, "It is harder for a rich man to enter the kingdom of heaven than a camel to go through an eye of a needle." In that particular instance the disciples were very perplexed. They said, "Lord who then can be saved?" Jesus responded by revealing to them, "With man it is impossible, but with God all things are possible." Heaven is infinitely beyond the reach of sinful men. Men need God to do the impossible. And God has accomplished this through Christ and His vicarious death and resurrection. It is all solely by grace. Deny Christ and it is impossible for an imperfect man to be accepted into a perfect heaven. One must have their imperfections and sins removed by the cross of God's Son.

The gospel offers the grace of God, peace with Him, and salvation freely given to the sinner (Romans 1:16-17, 10:15; Acts 20:24; Ephesians 1:13, 6:15). The law is distinct from the gospel but not separate, there is a unity within the diversity. Distinct but not separate. Both the law and gospel are in the whole of scripture. The two pertain to men and women and must be taught side by side with distinction within the oneness of scripture. Christians are to uphold the law with zeal and with truth through the grace and the power of the Holy Spirit. Some contemporary Christians believe the law is not to be upheld. They argue that we do not need to do the commandments in today's dispensation. These are antinomians. *Anti* means: against. The definition of *noumos*: Law. Hence an antinomian is against the law. If there is no moral law, there can be no hell and no punishment for lawbreakers. If the law is gone, you get rid of the absolute standards of right and wrong. You also get rid of hell, and you get rid of the need of the Savior too. If we are not lawbreakers we do not need to be saved.

The Life of a Christian

To live a life of obedience before God's face you must:

1. Admit that the flesh is weak (Matt. 26:41).
2. Pray for power and wisdom to overcome temptation and sin.
3. Avoid instruments, places, people, and circles that tempt you and where you previously fell.
4. Keep your focus on Jesus and His victory (1 Corinthians 15:56; Hebrews 12:1-2).

The church of Jesus Christ has plenty of programs, plenty of buildings, books and trinkets. But what we need most are trained mounted troops of God. Soldiers trained for sudden, daily charge against the gapping breaches in the enemies line opened daily by the word of God. The church has advanced through slow, pounding bombardments as it has opened hospitals, orphanages, outreaches and care centers. We must become loving troops: aggressive, compassionate, merciful, and unlimbering the great theological guns from the portholes of the churches. The great gospel weapons: The pounding of the truth of justification and lifting high the flag of the triune God must be our goal. Exalting the person of Christ our Prophet, Priest, and King should be our passion. He is the unstoppable weapon of the church: Jesus Christ.

Christians must become impassioned disciples to run with Jesus. Our moral duty is to put off all the excuses, indifference, sloppiness, slothfulness, slouchiness, laziness, and sluggishness. One can't be a Christian sluggard. A Christian can't afford to be droopy, duff, or negligent, but diligent in obedience and worship. It is about honoring God as God.

If you are weak and weary:

- Pray to God for power and grace.
- Praise and glorify God Almighty.
- Hence, if you are battle weary: Pray and praise.

The Old Rugged Cross

Jesus was nailed to a wooden cross to die for all His beloved. Jesus was persecuted, hounded, arrested, and Rome applied all manner of torment on Him. They crucified the Lord of glory. The crowds of evildoers scoffed and jeered. The pagan soldiers brandished spears and shook their fists and took His clothes. The crowd was hateful and cruel when they mocked the innocent Son of God. Jesus died because of men breaking God's moral law. That is love, real love. Love rose up Christ from the dead after it fastened Him to the cross. God Himself, unlimited, all conquering, all-consuming, infinite, eternal, omnipotent humbled Himself to die by the hands of men. That is a love that suffers long. This should motivate all believers to follow hard after the moral commandments of our Lord God.

> You have a few... who have not defiled their garments; and they shall walk with Me in white, for they are worthy (Revelation 3:4).

> Now to Him who is able to keep you from stumbling, and to present you faultless before the presence of His glory with exceeding joy. To God our Savior, Who alone is wise, be glory and majesty, dominion and power, both now and forever. Amen. (Jude 24-25).

This boundless love of that old rugged cross should motivate us to:

1. Evangelize the lost.
2. Glorify God everyday.
3. Follow God's word: Obey God's commandments.

> For You have delivered my soul from death. Have You not kept my feet from falling, that I may walk before God in the light of the living? (Psalms 56:13).

> My sheep hear My voice, and I know them, and they follow Me. And I give them eternal life, and they shall never perish; neither shall anyone snatch them out of My hand. My Father, who has given them to Me, is greater than all; and no one is able to snatch them out of My Father's hand (John 10:27-29).

The Certain Epistemological Foundation

One must have an epistemological foundation that is indubitable and universal to make sense out of human experience and ethics. Only Christianity offers elemental philosophical starting points for the intelligibility of the human experience. A young man told me that he questioned his faith because he read a book that claims that Jesus never existed. I told him I have dozens of books that make that same contention and they are fallacious because without Jesus Christ one cannot have the mandatory preconditions for the logic and morals the authors utilize while making their arguments. And the evidence is overwhelming that Jesus lived, died, and rose again. It's easy for anyone to attack Christ and make empty assertions. But it is impossible for those skeptics to supply the *a priori* philosophical environment for the invariant, universal, transcendent laws of logic and immutable, universal, transcendent moral laws. Only an all-knowing, omnipotent, and immutable God can. Hence those who argue against Christianity presuppose it and depend on the preconditions that only Christianity can provide.

No one can make sense of anything in the world without presupposing the existence of God. When one attempts to construct a worldview on anything but Christianity, one will find, under philosophical scrutiny, he cannot justify or account for anything in the cosmos. The person who denies the existence of God uses logic and reason to articulate his disbelief. Yet, he cannot justify the use of the necessary, nonmaterial, non-concrete, and universal laws of logic. God is inescapable. When anyone attempts to escape the truth that God exists, he falls into a trap that he cannot get out of. This point is well made in Van Til's fantastic illustration of a man made of water, who is trying to climb out of the watery ocean by means of a ladder that is made of water. He can't get out of the water for he has nothing to stand on. And without God, one cannot make sense of anything. The atheist has nothing to stand on, grip or climb.

Employing logic to disprove Almighty God is like

attempting to drain the Pacific Ocean using a hose that has the water turned on high. You can't drain an ocean with the water running. You are only adding to your problem. Thus those who attempt to refute God's existence are only adding to their problem. Their negation of Christianity presupposes the truth of Christianity. Non-Christian thought is self-rebutting and undercuts what it attempts to enumerate. Anti-theistic thought lacks epistemic justification. The only true standard would be one that has an all-knowing, unchanging, and all-powerful source. This can only be God. Substitution of atheistic epistemological standards in place of triune theistic standards is intelligible only on the presupposition of triune theism. Thus, anti-Christian epistemologies self-destruct.

Be Merciful to Those Who Doubt

Many people are afraid of doubt. Yet doubt presupposes God and His revealed word. Doubt employs the laws of logic and morality. God is the required precondition for logic and morality, thus doubt presupposes the triune God. This is good news if you have passing doubts about Christianity. It is also a tool we can utilize in our witness to those stuck in doubt. We should minister to doubters by:

    A. Praying for them.
    B. Praying with them.
    C. Showing them what scripture teaches about God and His moral law.
    D. Caring for them.

Those who have gone beyond doubting to walking the road to destruction, the Bible calls us to try to "snatch them from the fire." We must do the work of evangelists and grab them and pull them out of the path of hell by sharing with them the law and the gospel. Calvin said, "When there is a danger of fire, we do no hesitate to snatch away with force those who desire rescue."

Always remember the anti-theist and materialist cannot account for the laws of logic and fixed ethical standards. No one has ever stumbled over a law of logic in their child's room or threw one in a blender to add zip to an energy drink. One cannot touch, taste or see a nonmaterial law. Yet one must use them to make anything intelligible. Only with a presuppositional commitment to God can one make sense out of anything in the cosmos. Pollster George Barna discovered in 2005 that only one out of every six American adults admitted that they decide their moral choices based on the Bible. Only a little more than one third believe that moral truth is absolute. This is one reason for the theme and tone of this book. Without affirming absolute universal moral truth we may see more Holocausts, environmental disasters, and atrocities in war.

The Motivation for Charity

> And the King will answer and say to them,
> "Assuredly, I say to you, inasmuch as you did it to
> one of the least of these My brethren, you did it to
> Me" (Jesus).

The only immovable and consistent motivation for helping others is God. Ontologically we treat others with dignity and care because humans are created in the image of God. An attack on a man or woman is also an attack against the living God. Therefore issues that are built on the sanctity of life are grounded on the notion that man is created by God and made in His image. Human rights and liberty oriented democracy can only be secured on that basis. Deny God and one has no ultimate warrant for the liberty and the rights that people have in free societies.

Jesus Christ is the best example of ethical benevolence that this world has ever seen. Most of the hospitals and orphanages have been built by Christians and not skeptics and atheists.

Atheist Robert Ingersoll was once told by the famous preacher Henry Ward Beecher that he saw a poor crippled man beat up and thrown into a pile of filth and mud by a large brawny thug. Ingersoll responded: "What a brute he was!" Others listening agreed. "Yes," said Beecher, rising up with his fiery eyes on the skeptic. "Yes and Ingersoll, you are that man. The human soul is lame, but Christianity, that which you regularly attack, gives crutches to those crippled and a way to stay out of filth. But it is your teachings that knock these crutches from under it and leave the helpless wreck in the slough of despondency." Ingersoll's system of unbelief could not supply the conditions or the motivation to help the lame and keep men out of moral muck and mire.

The Aim

To have a fulfilled and joyful life one must aspire to live as a moral person for the glory of God. A world focused on itself cannot satisfy your soul. NFL Quarterback Tom Brady at age 28, after winning his third Super bowl ring, in November of 2005 admitted that "there must be more." There is and it is found in the moral Lawgiver: God Almighty. A 15th century English prayer is a good way to aim our lives:

> *God be in my head and in my understanding;*
> *God be in my eyes and in my looking;*
> *God be in my mouth and in my speaking;*
> *God be in my heart and in my thinking;*
> *God be at my end and in my departing.*

NOTES

1. Doug Wilson, *Wilson and Barker Debate Audio Tape* (Covenant Media: Irvine, CA).

2. Friedrich Nietzsche, *Thus Spake Zarathustra* (London, England: Dent & Sons, 1957), p. 79.

3. C.S. Lewis, *Surprised by Joy* (NY: Harcourt, Brace & Co.,1955), p. 213.

4. Edward Carpenter, *Common Sense About Christian Ethics* (NY: Macmillan, 1962), p. 27.

5. John P. Koster, Jr., *The Atheist Syndrome* (Brentwood, TN: Wolgemuth & Hyatt, 1989), p. 33.

6. Otto Von Bismarck, *1,911 Best Things Anybody Ever Said* (NY: Random House, 1988), p. 232.

7. Kurt Baier, *The Moral Point of View: A Rational Basis of Ethics* (NY: Ithaca, 1958), p. 314.

8. Will Marxsen, *New Testament Foundations for Christian Ethics* (Minneapolis, MN: Fortress Press, 1993), p. 312.

9. Charles Taylor, *The Ethics of Authenticity* (Cambridge, MA: Harvard University Press, 1991), p. 27.

10. Bertrand Russell, *Why I Am Not A Christian* (NY: Simon and Schuster, 1964), p. 200.

11. Ross and Kathryn Petras, *Stupid Celebrities: 500 of the Most Idiotic Things Ever Said by Famous People* (Kansas City, MO: McMeel Publishing, 1998), p. 54.

12. Benedictus Spinoza, *Ethics* (London, UK: Dent & Sons), pp. 177-178.

13. Craig Boldman, *Every Excuse in the Book: 714 Ways to Say it's not My Fault* (New York: MJF Books, 1998), p. 94.

14. C.S. Lewis: Martindale and Root, Editors, *The Quotable Lewis* (Wheaton, Il: Tyndale House, 1989), p. 59.

15. Thomas Morris, *Making Sense of It All* (Grand Rapids, MI: Eerdman, 1992), p. 211.

16. R.C. Sproul, *If There's a God, Why Are There Atheists?* (Wheaton, IL: Tyndale, 1978), p. 132.

17. P. Andrew Sandlin, *We Must Create A New Kind of Christian* (Vallecito, CA: Chalcedon Publication, 2000), p. 16.

18. Robert Audi, General Editor, *The Cambridge Dictionary of Philosophy, Second Edition* (Cambridge, UK: Cambridge Press 1999), p. 586.

19. Ibid., Audi, *The Cambridge Dictionary of Philosophy*, p. 284.

20. Norman Geisler, *Baker Encyclopedia of Christian Apologetics* (Grand Rapids, MI: Baker Books, 2000), pp. 414-416.

21. Carl Henry, Editor, *Wycliff Dictionary of Ethics* (Peabody, MA: 2000), p. 432.

22. Geddees McGregor, *Introduction to Religious Philosophy* (Boston, MA Mifflin, 1959), pp. 117-119.

23. John Barret, *Treatise of the Covenant quoted in Ernest Keran's The Grace of Law: A Study of Puritan Theology* (Norgan, PA: Soli Deo Gloria 1999), p. 48.

24. P.N. Ure, *Justinian and His Age* (Westport, CT: Greenwood Press, 1979) pp. 7-8.

25. Laura Schlessinger, *How Could You Do That? The Abdication of Character, Courage, and Conscience* (NY: Harper Collins, 1998), p. 142.

26. Prajnan Bhattacharya, *Hindu's Risk Health for Holiness* (Las Vegas, NV Review Journal, May 14, 2002, Associated Press), p. 7B.

27. John Calvin, *Sermons on the Ten Commandments, Edited and Translated by B.W. Farley* (Grand Rapids, MI: Baker Books, 1980), p. 68.

28. USA Today Newspaper: *News brief* (Mc Lean, VA: 6/3/02), p. 8A.

29. Andrew Ferguson, *The Sexologists Soldier On* (Las Vegas, NV: Las Vegas Review Journal, 6/7/02), p. 11B.

30. Rush Limbaugh, *See, I Told You So* (NY: Pocket Books, 1993), p. 85.

31. James Patterson and Peter Kim, *The Day America Told the Truth* (NY: Plume, 1992), p. 201.

32. John Frame, *Five Views of Apologetics, Steven Cowan, Editor* (Grand Rapids, MI: Zondervan, 2000), p. 226.

33. Benjamin Franklin, *Franklin: The Autobiography* (New York: Vintage Books, 1987), pp. 80-81.

34. Anthony Weston, *A Practical Companion to Ethics* (NY: Oxford University Press, 1997), p. 15.

35. Robert Morey, *The New Atheism* (Minn., MN: Bethany House, 1986), p. 63.

36. Viktor Frankl, *The Doctor and the Soul: Introduction to Logo Therapy* (NY: Knopf, 1982), p. 21.

37. Mark Twain, *The Mysterious Stranger* (NY: Dover Publishing, 1992), p. 52.

38. Sandy Thompson, *Whatever Happened to Basic Human Rights?* (Las Vegas, NV: Las Vegas Sun, 7/7/02), p. 30.

39. Louis Rene Beres, *In Maiming Israeli Bodies, Bombers Maim the Soul* (Las Vegas, NV: Las Vegas Review Journal, 5/28/02), p. 7B.

40. Geddees McGregor, *Introduction to Religious Philosophy* (Boston, MA: Mifflin, 1959), pp. 118-119.

41. Paul Rabinow, *The Foucault Reader* (NY: Random House, 1984), p. 346.

42. John Muether, *So Great a Salvation* (Phil., PA: Modern Reformation, Vol.10, Nu. 3. May/June 2001), p. 14.

43. Ibid., Sproul, *If There's a God, Why Are There Atheists?*, p. 133.

44. Jimmy Carter, *Living Faith* (NY: Random House, 1996), p.128.

45. Linda and Richard Eyrne, *Teaching Your Children Values* (NY: Simon and Schuster, 1993), p.13.

46. Charles Colson, *How Now Shall We Live* (Wheaton, IL: Tyndale, 1999), pp. 199-200.

47. David Frost, *The Americans* (NY: Avon Books), p. 89.

48. Thomas Watson, *The Ten Commandments* (Carlisle, PA: Banner of Truth, 1692), p. 46.

49. Ibid., John Calvin, *Sermons on the Ten Commandments*, p. 76.

50. Judge Joseph A. Wapner, *A View From The Bench* (NY: Simon and Schuster, 1987), p. 249.

51. Ibid., Carter, *Living Faith*, p.132.

52. Max Dimont, *Jews, God and History* (Nashville, TN: Nelson, 1998), p. 45.

53. Charisma, *Shari'ah Law Under Review in Ontario After Outcry by Human-Rights Groups* (Strang Publications, Lake Mary, FL: 12/04), p. 114.

54. B. Russell, *Religion and Science* (Oxford Press: NY, 1997), p. 223.

55. William Bennett, *Book of Virtues: A Treasury of Great Moral Stories* (Simon & Schuster, NY 1993), p. 133.

56. Ibid., p. 133.

57. James Q. Wilson, *The Moral Sense* (Free Press, NY 1998), p. 5.

58. Ibid., p. 5.

59. Ibid., p. 251.

60. Bennett, Ibid., p. 223.

61. Ibid.

62. Wallis, Claudia, *Time Magazine: Evolution Wars* (Time Warner: NY 8-15-05), p. 29.

63. Ibid., p. 30.

64. Ibid., p. 30.

65. Ibid., p. 31.

MICHAEL A ROBINSON

Printed in the United States
75414LV00002B/61-159